MW00931939

CHANGING CHURCH

It's Never Too Late

GALEN WOODWARD

WESTBOW®
PRESS
A DIVISION OF THOMAS NELSON
& ZONDERVAN

Copyright © 2014 Galen Woodward.

All rights reserved. No part of this book may be used or reproduced by
any means, graphic, electronic, or mechanical, including photocopying,
recording, taping or by any information storage retrieval system
without the written permission of the publisher except in the case
of brief quotations embodied in critical articles and reviews.

Scriptures taken from the Holy Bible, New International Version®, NIV®.
Copyright © 1973, 1978, 1984, 2011 by Biblica, Inc.™ Used by permission
of Zondervan. All rights reserved worldwide. www.zondervan.com The
"NIV" and "New International Version" are trademarks registered in
the United States Patent and Trademark Office by Biblica, Inc.™

WestBow Press books may be ordered through booksellers or by contacting:

WestBow Press
A Division of Thomas Nelson & Zondervan
1663 Liberty Drive
Bloomington, IN 47403
www.westbowpress.com
1 (866) 928-1240

Because of the dynamic nature of the Internet, any web addresses or
links contained in this book may have changed since publication and
may no longer be valid. The views expressed in this work are solely those
of the author and do not necessarily reflect the views of the publisher,
and the publisher hereby disclaims any responsibility for them.

Any people depicted in stock imagery provided by Thinkstock are
models, and such images are being used for illustrative purposes only.
Certain stock imagery © Thinkstock.

ISBN: 978-1-4908-2035-4 (sc)
ISBN: 978-1-4908-2034-7 (hc)
ISBN: 978-1-4908-2036-1 (e)

Library of Congress Control Number: 2013923046

Printed in the United States of America.

WestBow Press rev. date: 02/26/2014

Contents

Foreword

Talk to any pastor, and they'll tell you that there is no greater calling in the world than leading in the local church. Talk to them a little longer and they'll tell you there's nothing more rewarding. Talk to them even longer and they'll let you in on the fact that there's nothing more challenging!

As I've said for years: leadership is brutiful. There's a brutal side to it, and there's a beautiful side to it. The difficult nature of leadership, especially in the local church, comes in finding the balance between the ups and the downs. The challenge is continuing to move forward with what God has called us to do when we come up against difficulties we did not expect.

Human beings are creatures of habit. But few things can kill progress faster than habit. It's when we find ourselves stuck in those habits – stuck in those ruts – that we need a solution. It's not an easy solution. But it's a solution that can revolutionize our life and our leadership. And it can be found in one word: change.

Galen Woodward knows all about change. He understands how crucial change is, and he understands how difficult it is to implement. He has struggled in the shallows of sameness and he has experienced the thrill of riding on the crest of change. And in this book, he helps leaders embrace the reality that change doesn't have a timestamp.

When it comes to change, too many leadership books talk about the growth that emerges from it without looking at the reality of what it takes to live through it. But few books tackle the truth as head-on as this book – that the conflict that results from change is difficult, daunting, and can become disabling. But it's not impossible. In fact, without the challenge of change, we cannot grow into the leaders God wants us to become. It is through the struggle of changing that we experience the success of changing; it is through the trials that we discover the triumphs.

Through this book, Galen gives readers an inside look at the ups and downs of his journey. This isn't a five-step process on how to immediately change your church. It's not a self-help book to improve your leadership overnight. This book talks about the real and the raw of leading the local church in today's culture. It's a practical look at leadership in the trenches by one of the great men of God who has been there.

No matter where you are in your leadership; no matter how long you've been in the game, Galen Woodward will help you discover the truth that when it comes to Changing Church...It's Never Too Late!

Ed Young
Senior Pastor, Fellowship Church
Author, The Creative Leader

Endorsements

When I opened the manuscript on this book I was immediately drawn in. I felt like I had front seats in the life of a great pastor's incredible journey. Pastor Galen's writing style is transparent and relatable. He describes in detail the experiences that are rarely talked about in the life of a seasoned Pastor. He's also honest about the personal emotional roller coaster that goes along with those experiences. This book is a great read for pastors, teams and church members. Thank you, Pastor Galen, for sharing this amazing story of pain and purpose, faith and triumph.

Kevin Gerald
Senior Pastor, Champions Centre

Cultures change. People change. Too often churches get caught in a rut and refuse to change to meet the needs of the people of their day. This book is a must-read for every pastor and every believer who wants to affect their world. I have watched Galen and Kay and I've witnessed the journey that has made their church an influential force in our nation. Changing Church will inspire you to reach beyond what you see today and into the God-inspired dream that He has placed in your heart.

J. Don George
Founding Pastor, Calvary Church

My father, who is a veteran of two foreign wars, told me he did not want to be led into battle by any man that had never been shot…or at least shot at. Behind Pastor Galen Woodward's voice, it's easy to hear the miles on his odometer. Someone is always talking about a writer who "tells it like it is." That's fine, but first they have to KNOW how it is. From legalism to religiosity to genuine miracles, Galen has learned what it means to lead with joy when it's a "long, hot, smelly ride" and to keep his humility when the blessings are falling like rain. This is a guy who knows what it means to get shot at. This is a guy I'm willing to listen to.

Mark Rutland
President of Global Servants

Watching one of the fastest growing churches in America is so much fun, but what did it take to get there? The stories of leadership struggles, discouragement, failure, losing heart on your calling, and dreams, is what I didn't see. This literary piece of genius shows us the behind-the-scenes walking with, and listening to, the Holy Spirit as you obey His call in failure and success. I am grateful to Pastor Galen for giving me a true biblical perspective on what it takes to believe and build a marriage, a home, and a Christ-centered ministry.

Shannon O'Dell
Senior Pastor, Brand New Church

God uses the church to reach the world. For church leaders, this process can be both the cause of greatest pain and the source of most extraordinary joy.

In his book, Changing Church, Galen Woodward shares the personal story of his journey leading Copper Pointe Church through dark valleys of dissent and division to victorious mountaintops of unity and fulfilled purpose.

As I read this book, I was motivated, stirred and challenged. Get your copy, read with intent, and be prepared to be inspired!

Dr. Dave Martin
Author of The 12 Traits of the Greats

Dedication

This book is dedicated to our church staff at Copper Pointe
Church who embraced a new vision with passion. My sincere
thanks to each one who was willing to make the change.

Acknowledgements

I would like to express my sincere gratitude to my wife Kay and my three sons Dustin, Jonathan and Brandon Woodward. Without you this story could not be told.

Thank you to Kay Woodward, Jonathan Flores, Laine Brunetto and Brandon Harwell who provided much support and many hours of feedback and assistance in the editing, proofreading and design.

Also, Jose Cuellar, Tara Kienzel, Bryan Pettet, Cherise Roepcke, Mike Snapp and Tammy Stidworthy for their help in starting the process of making this book a reality.

And finally my deepest appreciation goes out to the great people of Copper Pointe Church, with whom I get to share God's Word each week and who are faithfully committed to winning a young generation.

Introduction

This book is written for four groups of people: Pastors, leaders, church volunteers and church attenders -- in other words, for Church People.

This is a story of change. Without question we all recognize the need for change in various areas of our lives. What has become so fascinating to me is how we can see the glaring need for change in our personal lives, at work and also within the church and yet avoid it at all cost.

I think the reason why is because change challenges our identity. It threatens our personal habits, values and attitudes, even dysfunctional ones. To change means letting go of deeply held values and ideas that have been taught to us by the people we love the most – parents, a teacher, a relative or a pastor. To discard some part of their teaching that has so defined us seems unthinkable, disrespectful and even wrong.

To disrupt these patterns of traditions for the average person is a devastating thing; our mind tells us that something is not right. It's the fear that this new way or method is going to lead us down a wrong path.

The sad fact is, most people will fight change until they reach their misery threshold and we can't take the pain anymore. So we change only after everything has crumbled under our feet and we are now forced to change for any hope of survival.

Have you ever really thought about why tradition is such a powerful thing? It is because as human beings we like to have patterns and order in our lives. We want things to be the way they have always been – in our family structure, our communities, or in our churches. We get used to a pattern from our childhood and associate it with comfort, safety and the absolute right way of doing things, so why change? The common attitude is, I like things just as they are. This kind of thought process can lead us down a long road of problems, missed opportunities and even a wasted life.

Leading change is a frustrating thing for leaders because you can't always paint the future with brilliant clarity for others to have the confidence to follow. Most people aren't willing to go into the future by faith of what could be, but to stay in the secure reality of the present. We all know that great advancements never happen by remaining in a state of rest. In other words, being caught in a rut of stale traditions.

Isaac Newton discovered three laws of motion that certainly apply to leading any organization.

1) The natural state of an object is at rest.
2) A moving object must overcome resistance.
3) Motion produces friction.

It sounds like he was describing the workings of the local church. In leading a long-established church, leaders will constantly face these same three challenges: natural inertia, resistance, and conflict.

> Inertia is a tendency to do nothing or to remain unchanged. This is when a church or business has stopped growing and has come to a complete standstill.

> Resistance is the refusal to accept or comply with something; the attempt to prevent something by action or argument. This is when employees or church members become disgruntled with a new direction, openly spreading negativity about the new vision, the direction, and the leader of the organization.

> Friction is a force that holds back the movement of a moving object. This is when people of an organization or church will rise up with violent opposition against leadership, which leads to a strike, a mass walk-out or church split.

Thousands of well-established traditional churches are trapped in a state of rest, remaining the same size for many years with small impact in their community. Something has to change but the moment you lead a significant change you will be met by resistance and friction.

Leading change is what few leaders are willing to do.

This is why there is no shortage of discouraged leaders pastoring well-established churches that have found themselves trapped by deep-rooted traditions. The common consensus of most leaders is the belief that change causes too much disruption and it's not worth all the resistance and friction they will face. That's why eighty percent of churches across America are two hundred or less in attendance. That statistic should make every Christian grieve over the weakness of the Western Church. So many long-standing congregations have found themselves ministering to the same people week after week, year after year, and my question is, why would any of us think it's OK to allow our church to remain in a state of rest? The answer, there are few leaders willing to take on the task of transformation in the established church because of the strong opposition they will endure through the process.

No wonder so many young pastors are opting for planting a church or developing unconventional type ministries rather than taking on an old traditional local church.

Today, much is being written about church planting, and great success stories are springing up all across the nation. I have the highest respect for pastors who take on that enormous challenge. But what about pastors taking well-established churches and congregations that are unwilling to change, churches that are caught on dead center and cannot produce any kind of growth? I found myself in this exact spot, completely lost and overwhelmed in what to do. There seems to be so little guidance for leaders who are desperately in need of transforming an old model into a new model. God calls leaders to advance His Kingdom and many times it will be at a great price. But this is a fact: If a new breed of spiritual reformers don't rise up and turn the tide of the American church we are going to lose this nation spiritually.

After thirty years of experience, I want to give you a first-hand look of what it's like to be caught in religious traditions, pastoring a dead, lifeless church for fourteen years, and how we transformed this seventy-five-year-old church into a growing, creative, life-giving church. I want to expose the religiosity that controls so many churches, what stops growth, and what destroys so many pastors and leaders.

If you've been in church for any length of time you will identify with what I'm about to share. You will be amused and at the same time your heart will break by the story of church people.

Changing Church will be the greatest adventure of your life. Join me in this journey of self-evaluation, and become a reformer of the next generation!

Chapter 1

The "Brutiful" Side of Ministry

(Thanks, Ed Young!)

Dreams really do come true. I wasn't convinced of this for the longest time. I believed anyone could dream but only the highly gifted, extremely intelligent, or incredibly lucky would ever be able to say, "I'm living the dream." Well, I'm neither gifted nor highly intelligent and have never considered myself lucky, though somehow I've found myself in a place that has exceeded my expectations. To dream a dream is one thing, but living the dream is spectacular. It was late on a Friday night when, for the first time, I realized that I was in fact living the dream. The very thing I had longed for had actually become reality. In fact, it exceeded anything I had dreamed of as a young man.

We had just completed a very long and difficult church relocation project, and the next day was our grand opening. All day long, hundreds of volunteers were franticly working in an effort to get everything cleaned and organized. Teams of people had been there all day getting ready for the biggest day in the history of our church. I thought about all of the wonderful people in our congregation who played a part in making this dream come true. I'm not sure why, but God has blessed me to pastor the greatest people on earth, who are loving, godly, committed, faithful servants and who love the lost!

After a long and exhausting day, and after everyone had gone home, I realized I was the last person in the building. As I approached the front doors I couldn't bring myself to leave. Finding myself lingering in the front entry I turned around and started walking. I walked through the foyer that flowed into the atrium and on to the auditorium. I strolled slowly, soaking in and enjoying the moment of absolute solitude, which is something I had not experienced in months. I will cherish that moment for the rest of my life. As I walked through the building I felt like

God was walking right beside me. It was truly a sacred moment. I stood there shaking my head in disbelief and wondered to myself how I got here. Tears flowed down my face. The only words that would come out of my mouth were, "He is able to do far beyond all that we ask or think." This was a verse I had memorized as a young boy and quoted many times, but this was really the first time I quoted it with real understanding. I was standing in a new multi-million dollar building that was opening the next day.

That weekend we had over four thousand in attendance and several hundred gave their lives to Christ. The next weekend we baptized just over two hundred people. Those two weekends made me understand that dreams are not simply for those the world deems as exceptional but for everyone who has a dream.

I want to tell you a story about a dream. All of us have a dream but I wonder why is it that some dreams come true while many others never become more than a fleeting fantasy. When we are young our dreams are untamed and uninhibited. Nothing is unreachable and we don't even know the meaning of fear. Then, as time clicks by, age has accelerated faster than you'd anticipated and you are now challenged by the problems and difficulties of the adult world. Somehow the dream begins to fade. It sits on the shelf being ignored as you continue your busy daily routine. You find that the dream of success somehow has slipped through your fingers. Whether you are a business person, church leader, church volunteer, pastor, or someone still figuring out their direction in life, I want to assure you that your dream is not too elusive or too far out of reach. I believed time had passed me by and wondered why my dream had not come true. I want to share my story with you so that you can discover, just like I did, that your dream is right around the corner.

In The Beginning

I graduated from Southwestern Assemblies of God University and eight months later I married my beautiful wife Kay. I was 23 and she was 19. We had just become youth pastors in Albuquerque, New Mexico. I was from west Texas and Kay from Mobile, Alabama. Kay grew up with her family, spending her summers at their beach house in Gulf Shores overlooking the beautiful white sand and the ocean waves of the Gulf of Mexico. When we pulled into Albuquerque it was 105 degrees and everything looked scorched and brown. All she could say was, "It's so brown. Where is the grass and where are the trees?" You could literally see up to a hundred miles away. There was great resistance from this 19-year-old who was moving halfway across the United States from her family. If that wasn't bad enough, we were moving to the desert. I told her to look on the bright side and pointed out that there was a whole lot of beach…just without the water. She didn't find that humorous at all. Since we had no other job offers, I convinced her that we should accept the position. I told her that we would only stay for a year, and she reluctantly agreed.

Little did we know that this was to be the beginning of a lifelong adventure.

We were young and filled with passion and energy. We started our youth ministry with seven students. I gave it all I had. I was going to the high school campuses every week and had a daily radio program on a new contemporary Christian station that gave us tremendous exposure. In the next few years we saw incredible growth. Kay and I loved every minute of youth ministry. The years passed quickly.

Twelve years later our senior pastor took another position and we were voted in as the church's new pastors.

The day we were voted in was the most exciting day of my life. I was ready to turn the world upside down. That day as I stood on the stage with my wife and our three young boys receiving a standing ovation, it felt like the whole world was at my fingertips. The future was limitless. It couldn't get any better than this. This was a church in which I had spent twelve years. My best friends were in this place. The staff members were people I knew and with whom I worked well. Students that I had led to the Lord and who had grown up in our youth ministry were now raising their families in the church. Many of them were now in leadership and some were on the church board. I knew everyone in the church. I loved them and they trusted me. This was a match made in heaven. Being in the midst of all these friends, I could not see anything but success and happiness on the horizon. What could go wrong?

Two years into our pastorate I was completely caught off guard. Call it naïve, immature or just plain stupid, but I was completely blindsided by what was about to take place.

A faction began to rise against me and the direction I was leading the church, primarily by a group of young men who prided themselves as intellectuals in regard to Scripture. They took great offense to the vision I had launched, "Win the lost at all cost." I was creating a culture of outreach that was foreign to the current culture of our church. I was shocked that anyone could find fault in what I believed was following the Great Commission.

But they began to build their case on the premise that discipleship should be our main focus.

They began to verbalize their concerns with many people. Their thought was that if we were to win the masses to Christ we would be unprepared to correctly disciple them. A ridiculous battle was brewing over the great "discipleship vs. evangelism" debate. What bothered me about this train of thought was that these church people had been together for many years. I'm talking about a group of Christians that had been attending our church for forty, fifty, and sixty years. These were not new believers and they were talking about simply stuffing themselves with more study of the Bible. These people had already been taught the Bible far beyond their capacity for obedience. I believed it was time to gather the troops, get beyond our four walls, and win the lost. They strongly believed it was the wrong direction for our church, and their mission was to set me straight. When I disagreed with them they accused me of not caring to teach deep, intellectual truths of God's Word. Their conversations with me were condescending and meant to make me feel less spiritual than themselves. They made it very clear that in their prayer gatherings God had given them the direction of the church and the direction I was leading was wrong. Immediately I realized I had found myself in the midst of a raging power struggle. These were good men but I was amazed at how quickly this turned vicious. It felt like I had been challenged to a duel of deadly weapons and only one contender would be standing in the end.

They slowly and effectively started planting their seed of dissension and they reinforced their cause by adding divisive statements such as, "If you really knew what was going on behind the scenes you would be shocked! But I'm not going to talk bad about the pastor." They certainly impressed others with their seemingly high level of spirituality by not being willing to talk about me. But they left them with the pondering question, "What is going on that we are unaware of? What do they know that they are not telling us?"

They were planting seeds of doubt. They left it up to the hearer's imagination, and of course their imaginations ran wild. As we all know, accusation is one of Satan's greatest weapons in the church.

This group was dividing the church slowly with each and every conversation. I could feel the tension growing among people, and yet I had no idea of what was really being spread. There is no worse feeling than knowing something terrible is happening and not knowing how to stop it.

People were choosing sides. Tension began to build. Vicious and ridiculous rumors started to spread. Accusations flew. It was like a spirit of confusion had swept over our congregation. People were angry, frustrated and confused and they didn't even know why. What I quickly realized is that most people don't care about lines of authority or what is true and right but they will defend and side with the person to whom they are the closest.

Division can quickly escalate through misunderstanding, gossip, dissatisfaction, dishonor, confusion, and pride. It may start in the minds of men and women, but the situation quickly gets energized by our spiritual enemy. This is when church conflict becomes extremely dangerous – when the need to be right overrides our highest call to keep love and unity in the Body of Christ.

King Solomon is known for his wisdom when two mothers came to him for help. They both had babies. One woman's baby had died and they were both claiming that the living baby was theirs. King Solomon said he was going to cut the living baby in half and give half of the baby to each of the mothers. (That's weird.)

One woman said, "Ok, cut it in half, I want my half." (That's disturbing!) The other woman said, "No, don't kill it – give it to the other woman." Solomon said the woman who wanted the baby to live was the real mother. The one who was willing to kill it for her own satisfaction could not be the real mother.

In the same way, people who are willing to risk killing the church in order to be right do not have the heart of God or a love for His Church.

What made this so difficult was that this faction was coming from a few disgruntled members in our own leadership, including a staff member. Instead of dismissing them from their leadership roles I was in hopes that things would get better. I knew that firing staff or dismissing board members could be very explosive in a time of unrest. I also knew that doing so would be the perfect excuse for them to start another church with a ready-made congregation.

This dissension went on for almost a year, and tremendous damage was done. It led to our church board putting into motion the steps of removing a few key leaders who were at the core of the disturbance.

During a Sunday morning service I announced the disciplinary action that had been taken. It was like pouring gasoline on a fire. A definite line had been drawn in the sand. The moment that service was over, one of the church members caught me by the arm declaring, "This church will not survive this and I will make sure of it. The doors of this building will be closed in six months." My young son, Dustin, was standing with me and witnessed this outburst of anger. He could tell that the words delivered me a crushing blow. I could see the horrified look on his face and so badly didn't want this to harden his heart toward ministry.

As a young and inexperienced pastor I was stunned how this kind of venom could actually flow from believers. Frustrations had reached a boiling point and I knew a church split was inevitable.

A church split is usually characterized by a large group of people, maybe 20 percent or more of the congregation, joining together to leave because of a disagreement. It's normal for every church to have a few people split from time to time, which is hard enough, but this split was mounting to include at least half of our congregation – that is a whole other experience.

Church Split Or Revival

I received a phone call from a great friend, Johnny Jernigan, who was traveling as an evangelist. He was confirming a scheduled four-day revival starting on Sunday. His call caught me completely off guard. The revival wasn't on our calendar and I didn't have any remembrance of such a conversation. He assured me we had booked the meeting and that it had been on his schedule for over a year. While on the phone I was thinking to myself that there couldn't be a worse time to have a revival. We are in the middle of a church split! This is a hostile crowd and no one is going to be in the mood for revival services. I was stuck. He had already bought his plane tickets so I told him to come and figured we would get the word out somehow.

That Saturday afternoon when Kay and I met him at the airport, immediately he detected that something was wrong. We were a bundle of nerves and we didn't hide it very well. Sunday morning the tension was so thick you could cut it with a knife. We made it through those four nights. He was the greatest encourager I had ever met. He was highly perceptive and understood the strain that the church was experiencing. Those four nights were amazing. He said that for the next several months he would be willing to come and preach every other week. I would preach Sunday mornings, he would preach Sunday and Monday nights, believing that God would bring healing in all of this turmoil.

Those services were really amazing. You could sense the presence of God. The group of church people that was upset always showed up but wouldn't come into the auditorium. They stood in the foyer and hallways, cornering people and building their case against church leadership. It was a recru ting campaign explaining to people why they should leave. Inside of the auditorium God's word was being preached. It was a soothing and a reassuring message telling us of God's promises even in the midst of a storm. In the hallways a different message was being heard.

I scheduled a board meeting on that Sunday night to assess how much damage had taken place thus far. That night one of the board members had become very agitated. It was apparent that he had entertained many conversations which had negatively affected him. In our meeting his temper flared. He seemed to be agitated with everything. He demanded that I stop this series of services with the evangelist, claiming his preaching was unbiblical. It was clear with whom he had been spending time. He continued to say that these meetings were clouding the current issues and that I needed to stop it that night! I refused and replied that I would not.

I was an emotional wreck walking out of that meeting and straight into the Sunday night service. Sitting on the front row, tears were streaming down my face uncontrollably. I knew walking out of that meeting there was no hope of holding this church together. I felt like God was a million miles away. I had been thrown to the wolves and God was nowhere to be found. I couldn't have been more wrong. That night the most amazing thing happened. It was at a level I had never experienced in my life.

There was a couple in our church, Dan and Karen. Dan had been a fireman and in the midst of battling a fire he was caught in a very dangerous situation that left him with a major injury to his leg. It left him crippled and he was forced to go on disability. He went through several surgeries with little success. The worst part of all was that he was in constant pain. He had tried medication, pain management therapy, and acupuncture, all to no avail. He couldn't get any relief. There were many nights when the pain was so severe that his wife would call me frantically asking for prayer. I went to his house many times praying for God to heal him and relieve his pain. Each time I would walk away agonizing for him, wishing so badly that God would do something. Dan was big and strong but could do nothing but sit in a chair or lie in bed tormented with pain. It had taken away his quality of life. This had gone on for ten years. His church attendance had become very sporadic because it was so difficult to get there and sit through a service. He loved church and wanted to be there more than anything. The Sunday night of the revival, he and his wife showed up.

The service began; the worship team had kicked off but all was not well. I certainly wasn't in the mood for church that night and my mind had drifted a million miles away. I knew my time here as pastor was running out quickly. My deep thoughts of gloom and despair were suddenly disrupted by Dan, who was on the far side of the auditorium acting strangely. He was walking back and forth, moving from side to side. His eyes caught mine and he stared straight at me. I was in the front row and I moved toward him. I noticed something out of the ordinary. His walker was up against the wall. He began walking toward me with no assistance. When he reached me he said, "Pastor, I think God just healed me."

The man of faith that I was, I said, "No way!" He said that he thought he was experiencing a hot flash at first but then realized the pain was gone. He had full range of motion in both of his legs. "I'm healed! God has healed me!"

I went home that night in total amazement. I lay in bed that night wondering if he was really healed. Was that some kind of emotional response? Did he want to be healed so badly that he was imagining that he was healed? The next day I picked up the phone several times to call him but each time I put it back down. What if his pain was back? What if he woke up and had to start using his walker again? We had announced it in front of everyone the previous night. I didn't call him because I couldn't take another disappointment. That Monday night I arrived early for our revival service. I stood in the foyer pacing back and forth like a caged animal, wringing my hands, waiting for them to arrive. My question remained. Was he still healed?

About that time their car pulled into the parking lot. He was driving, which was an unusual sight. They both got out of the car and started for the front doors. It didn't even look like Dan. He stood tall and straight and walked with no assistance. He had the walk of a strong young man. That night he volunteered to be one of the ushers who received the offering. As he walked down the aisle there wasn't a dry eye in the place.

This was an undeniable miracle. It was like something straight out of the New Testament.

I sat there shaking my head. In all of this confusion God shows up in a way that no one could have ever imagined. He came simply to say, "This is My church and I'm in charge of what happens here!"

Even when Satan throws his best punch, trying to destroy the church and drag Jesus' name through the mud, it's futile. Jesus declared that the gates of Hell will not prevail against His church. In my mind there was no doubt that God loves His church and will defend it to the end. But what I wasn't so sure of was me. Was God really going to see me through all of this? Would our family survive this? What if I didn't measure up in the eyes of God? Maybe I didn't pray enough. What if God was disappointed in me? What if all of this was my fault and I was just getting what I deserved? Sure, God cares about His church, but does He care about me? I was so focused on the problem and my personal pain that I couldn't even see God when He chose to magnificently reveal Himself in my greatest time of need. Isn't it strange that God can literally reveal himself to ensure hope and confidence and yet we still question His allegiance?

I can remember being a kid sitting in Sunday School and hearing all of the Old Testament stories of Israel wandering in the desert. For those forty years, God revealed Himself to them time after time. I remember the ten plagues, the parting of the Red Sea and water pouring out of a rock to quench their thirst. There was a cloud by day and a pillar of fire to guide them by night. God provided food for them every day and literally destroyed Jericho before their very eyes. After all of this, they still doubted God. Sitting in a Sunday School class I would think, "How stupid do you have to be to see these miracles and still fail to trust Him?" What I criticized passionately, in regard to the Israelites, was the very thing I was doing. In the biggest mess of my life, and when everything looked hopeless, God showed up in Biblical proportions to say, "I'm here! I'm right here in the midst of the storm – sitting beside you in the boat." I was so focused on the waves of destruction that all I could see was the storm instead of the Savior. I was still asking God, "Where are you? Why have you forsaken me?" I

> *I was so focused on the waves of destruction that all I could see was the storm instead of the Savior.*

was just like the Israelites. Isn't it interesting that in the most difficult times of our lives we become so focused on the problem that we can't see the miracle worker, Jesus Christ, the Son of the

Living God, the author and finisher of our faith, the Beginning and the End?

Still, all I could see was my quick descent to utter failure.

———◆———

Meanwhile, back at the church, everyone was excited for Dan. It seemed to dampen the disgruntled church people and their agenda. They were happy for Dan but they were angry that it happened during the revival that they so hated, and under my leadership with which they were in such opposition. It actually fueled their anger and they began to plot against me.

Healing Or Jewish Temple Split

In Luke chapter 6 Jesus has come on the scene with a new vision and direction for His church. He was using new methods that had never been seen before. Huge crowds were gathering on the outskirts of town, sitting on the hillside to listen to Him, instead of gathering in the synagogue. He taught creatively, using dirt, bread, children, animals, and everyday experiences to make his point. It was a paradigm shift of ministry. He was doing things that had never been done before. The teachers of the Law hated Him for it. He was disrupting two thousand years of synagogue (church) traditions.

So they invited Jesus to teach in the synagogue on the Sabbath. The Pharisees and teachers of the Law were looking for a reason to discredit Him. They knew He would do something unorthodox and hopefully they could expose Him as a fraud. They were right. As Jesus was speaking, He looked up and saw a man in the back of the room with a shriveled hand. He stopped in the middle of His teaching and called for him to come to the front of the synagogue.

Jesus told him to stretch out his hand and the moment he did his hand was totally healed. The Pharisees and teachers immediately responded, not by singing the praises of a miracle-working God, but by declaring that He had broken the Law. He had healed on the Sabbath. In Luke chapter 6 and verse 9, Jesus said to them, "I ask you, which is lawful on the Sabbath: to do good or to do evil, to save life or to destroy it?" He was showing them the idiocy of their legalism.

But they were furious and they began to discuss with one another what they might do to Jesus. They went out and plotted His destruction.

———•———

It is alarming to me that church people can be this spiritually blinded.

God shows up in the midst of their religious gathering; they see a man healed before their very eyes and all they can think about is how badly they hate Jesus for messing with their traditions. I'm convinced that there is nothing worse than a crowd of angry church people. I want to clarify myself: I'm not referring to fully devoted followers of Christ. I'm talking about "religious people." I'm talking about the church people who have created their own agenda. These were the people who were constantly confronting Jesus.

———•———

Within the next few weeks the church was split almost perfectly down the middle, and already they were making plans to start their own church. Almost overnight we had lost half our congregation, which included long-time members, board members, teachers, children's workers, and half of the church's income. The amount

15

of hate mail I received was unimaginable. The pain of their words cut deeply. They assured me with great pride that the church would never survive. And I knew they were right. It was like the aftermath of a war. Casualties were everywhere. The saddest thing of all was the new Christians who were caught in the middle who said, "If this is what Christians do, then we want no part of it."

For me, the pain became so great that I could feel myself slipping into depression. My heart ached. I never knew your heart could actually hurt. I had heard the term "a broken heart" and for the first time in my life, I experienced it. For weeks I had church people scheduling meeting after meeting to tell me why they were leaving the church. Each one wanted to take their personal jab – like one more low blow to take a little more life from me – tearing away at my self-worth. After two months of these meetings, every ounce of my self-confidence had been ripped from me. Those meetings so affected me that after a while my hands trembled uncontrollably. They had been very effective in convincing me that I was a total failure. I know this may sound strange, but I grieved as if a family member had died. It was the death of friendships with people who had become like family. It was the death of a dream along with the destruction of a church. Fourteen years we had invested into each other, and now our friendships had turned to hatred.

I searched my heart and my motives and could not figure out how all of this went so wrong. It made no sense.

One Sunday morning, as I was standing in the shower, I thought to myself that I couldn't do this again. There would be people coming to receive something from me, and I had nothing to give. How could I be such a failure? I had failed the church, my wife, and my kids. I couldn't lift my head from the embarrassment.

I withdrew from people, declaring that no one would ever hurt me like that again.

The trauma of these events brought me to the brink of a nervous breakdown. I was fighting to just get through another day. I was so traumatized, that I cried every day for over a year. It's hard to even explain what those Sundays were like after the church split. It was like a funeral service. The crowd was sparse and lightly scattered throughout the auditorium. People who had gone to church together for many years were now divided – being forced into making a decision to stay or to go.

Unfortunately, my story is not uncommon.

Chapter 2

Ministry and Warfare Are Synonymous

The battle rages everywhere. Church disputes, power struggles, conflicts, infighting, and church splits. This is one area Bible college never prepared me for. In fact, in all four years I never remember anyone ever talking about these kinds of struggles. When this happens, leaders feel so alone and congregations are left disillusioned. Who do you turn to? Who do you talk to?

There are days, even as a spiritual leader, that you don't even sense a hint of God's presence.

Today, as I reflect back upon so many difficult days, I'm reminded of God's faithfulness. When you're in the heat of the fight, it may not yet be clear, but God is always at work. He gives you exactly what you need to keep moving forward – whether you realize it or not.

> *When you're in the heat of the fight, it may not yet be clear, but God is always at work.*

The church staff was tremendously loyal and vowed to stay and rebuild. The only problem was that we couldn't figure out how we would continue paying their salaries with the huge financial hit we had just taken. Still to this day I don't understand how, but we never missed a salary check for any of our staff. Each of these staff members who walked alongside us through some of our darkest days hold a dear place in my heart and are still some of my closest friends today.

How blessed we have been to have families that love God, love the church and love us. Kay's parents, from Mobile, Alabama, and my parents, from Amarillo, Texas, were a tremendous support to us during this time. For the first few months after the church split they would alternate coming to Albuquerque to spend weekends with us. We often stayed up all night praying together and they did anything they could to offer encouragement. But mostly, their simply being with us was what we needed most. There were also two couples in the church with whom we had become very close. We spent tremendous amounts of time with these dear friends and even vacationed together. When our world came crashing down, they were with us every step of the way with the most encouraging words of love and support. I look back on that time and know that their friendships were divine and a gift for Kay and me.

We went to dinner with them every Friday night, and it became what we lived for. Their words and love were enough to help us fight through one more week. God brings wonderful blessings into our lives at just the right moment because He knows exactly what we always need. What I know today is that without them, I would have never survived the journey. Even when you don't see anything good, good things are happening. You just may not recognize it. In hard times, open your eyes. I mean, really open your eyes and you will see heaven's little gifts popping up all along the way – assuring you, it is all OK.

Have you ever wondered why church division is so painful? It's because the church is unlike any other institution on earth. For a pastor, it's his place of ministry, worship, social life, and occupation. On top of that, it doesn't just affect him, but it also directly affects the personal lives of each one of his family members. It's not just losing a job or changing churches. In one sweeping blow they lose almost everything. Many times it delivers such a crushing blow to the minister's family that they never fully recover.

The Schaeffer Institute of Church Leadership Development said that 35 to 40 percent of pastors leave the ministry after just five years of pastoring. A startling 1500 pastors leave the ministry each month due to moral failure, spiritual burnout, or contention in their churches. An alarming 50 percent of pastors' marriages will end in divorce. Eighty percent of seminary and Bible school graduates who enter the ministry will leave the ministry within the first five years. And 70 percent of pastors constantly fight depression. Most statistics say that 60 to 80 percent of those who enter the ministry will not still be in it 10 years later. And only a fraction will stay in the ministry as a lifetime career.

Church members are also traumatized by church divisions. Sad to say, many of them also never recover. We all know people who have been hurt by the church. It left them so bitter that they never return and tragically they raise their children outside of the church. Our country is filled with people who have had horrible experiences within the church.

Jesus identified a religious spirit that permeated the Pharisees of his day. Isn't it fascinating that Jesus' opposition was not from the pagans but from the religious? This is not uncommon and all leaders must be on guard for this attack.

Satan's Greatest Weapon, the Religious Spirit.

I want to take a moment and talk about this destructive spirit. Look with me at a story in 2 Kings 2. Elisha traveled to the city of Jericho to discover that the city was faced with a crisis. Their water was toxic and undrinkable. This poison had made the land barren and was causing widespread sickness and death, affecting people and animals as well as their crops. So Elisha does a very strange thing. Verse 21 says,

> Then he went out to the spring and threw the salt into it, saying, "This is what the Lord says: 'I have healed this water. Never again will it cause death or make the land unproductive.'"

This story in the Old Testament offers us a picture of the gospel where Jesus said, "I, Christ, heal that which is sick and diseased." He neutralizes the poisons that cause spiritual barrenness among the church.

So many churches today are debilitated because of a religious spirit. It is laced with legalism, outward appearances, and spiritual superiority.

Jesus Himself referred to these toxins as "the leaven of the Pharisees" in Matthew 16:11-12.

He told us that the Pharisees' religion looked good on the outside but was deadly on the inside and highly contagious.

A religious spirit may look spiritual on the outside but on the inside it is joyless, cynical, hypercritical, and prideful. This poison can spread rapidly and cause a church to be completely ineffective. It develops a harsh, judgmental attitude toward others, yet typically struggles with sinful habits that they cannot admit. A religious spirit will fight against progressive changes and new ideas that come from leadership. This is why many churches become irrelevant to society.

Churches that allow these attitudes become dangerously vulnerable to deception and will function in religious formality instead of functioning by the guidance of the Holy Spirit.

When church people refuse to shift with God from religious formality to Holy Spirit guidance, the church must find more flexible vessels that are willing to implement His changes. A religious spirit cannot go unchecked because once it is in power, hell is on the throne.

> *A religious spirit cannot go unchecked because once it is in power, hell is on the throne.*

This religious spirit ran rampant through our church. Like a weed it tried to take over a beautiful garden and kill its harvest. As a follower of Christ, whether a pastor, volunteer, ministry leader, teacher, elder, or deacon, this is a spirit that we must be aware of and capable of identifying. What makes this so difficult is that it will most likely flow through people who have long tenure in the church and carry great influence among much of the congregation.

You are able to discern a religious spirit before you see its destructive effects. You can sense it, feel it, and know it, but if you try to pin down the offenders by their words or deeds, you may be too late in stopping major damage.

Many times we put confrontation off because of intimidation. We second-guess our discernment. We are waiting for proof of their actions or maybe we think it will all work itself out. That's not leadership! This is the very reason we experienced a massive church split. I avoided the issues using all of these excuses. Now, with thirty years of pastoral experience, I want to help you identify this religious toxin. It doesn't abide in just some churches but in all churches. I'm sure the toxic church people I have encountered will be the very same kind of people that you encounter. I want to expose this spirit because it is Satan's number one attack against the Church.

The Warning Signs of a Religious Spirit

...believes it has the right plan and direction for the church.

...is on a mission to tear down what it believes is wrong.

...believes it does not need to listen to leadership because it can hear from God itself.

...immediately notices what is wrong with people or the church, rather than looking for what is right.

...loves to gather people for food and fellowship but always finds time to cast concern and doubt upon the church leadership.

...often says things like, "The pastor doesn't preach the Word" or "The church's priority is not right" or "I'm just not being fed" or "If I were in charge..."

...may feel as though they are truly closer to God than others, and their own ministry is more pleasing to God in comparison.

...will do things simply to be noticed as being highly spiritual. It's their way of control and power.

...tends to zero in on molehills and makes them into mountains.

...will overreact to immaturity in the body of Christ, claiming the whole church is not spiritual.

...will not fully commit to the leadership of the church because they do not measure up to their standards.

This behavior flies in the face of Biblical authority and leadership. This spirit is extremely prideful and wants to hide behind a religious facade in order to divide people and take control.

Solomon made a wise statement in Proverbs when he said, "Plans fail for lack of counsel, but with many advisers they succeed."

What great advice. There is nothing better than when godly people come together to plan for the future. I never make major decisions on my own but only after seeking the counsel of people I trust and in whom I believe. The advice of others has kept me from making so many rash and poor decisions. But the one with a religious spirit will not operate in love and unity or with the church's best interest in mind. They operate from an arrogant and prideful spirit that fights for their own personal agenda.

This constant inward contention is what brings so much stress and exhaustion to spiritual leaders.

I remember attending a statewide ministers' conference. We had just finished the morning session and the speaker had been phenomenal. We moved from the auditorium to the church gymnasium for lunch. Round tables were set up and we were to find a seat. Before they served the food they wanted to give everybody the opportunity to get to know one another. We were asked to take thirty minutes, go around the table, introduce ourselves and share a need. Then, everyone would join together in praying for them. One by one, pastors and their wives began sharing. The sharing quickly became very personal and emotional. It was a safe environment to share and vent frustrations. Tears were streaming down their faces as they talked about failures, disappointments, and painful conflicts with people in their congregations. Having recently gone through my own painful situation, my heart broke for them. I lifted my head as our group was praying and started looking around the room. It was the same at every table. Broken ministers were everywhere.

I left there that day very disillusioned. I thought, "Is this what I have to look forward to for the rest of my life?" I must admit, I walked away from that conference very discouraged. I was still reeling from my own ministry disaster and I certainly didn't have any answers for anyone else. As Kay and I drove home that afternoon I don't think either one of us said a word. We were both in deep thought. I don't know about Kay, but I was struggling with ministry in general and definitely didn't want to live like this any longer. My joy in life was gone. What was extremely disturbing to me was that I honestly couldn't remember the last time I had laughed. What had happened to me? I was battling something I did not understand. It wasn't until several years later that I came to understand that discouragement is just a part of ministry and life in general. There is no way around it. We will all experience it, so we must learn how to navigate through it and overcome it.

Dealing With Discouragement

Many people enter into ministry as if they're going to live out the rest of their lives in heavenly bliss because they are surrounded by fellow Christians and shielded from the harsh realities of the world.

We need to really think through the work of the ministry before we jump in with both feet. For ministers and church leaders, one of the biggest struggles we face is discouragement. Even the Apostle Paul was a victim of its enormous power. Discouragement had the potential to destroy the effectiveness of his ministry. He knew too well the deep pain that comes from working with people in the church. The very people he had poured into the most were the ones who turned on him and broke his heart.

The city of Corinth, which had been restored by Julius Caesar after being in ruins for a hundred years, was now the most liberal city in Europe.

Over 18 months Paul had labored day in and day out in this god-forsaken city. It was here that he built a great church and a great affection and love for its people. When you love people so profoundly, they have the potential to hurt you severely. Sin and spiritual disaster marked this church. All of the lashes that went across Paul's back, all of the stones thrown at him to blot out his life, didn't bring him the pain that he felt over the spiritual defection of the people into whom he had poured his life. It was more difficult than any other kind of suffering he had experienced. He had given them so much of himself, and had taught them so well, yet they were divided and selfish. They were disorderly and worldly. They fought with and sued one another. They took sexual advantage of each other. And they were filled with pride. Additionally, as if the sin and the spiritual scandals weren't enough, some false teachers came to Corinth, managing to organize members of the church into a mutiny against Paul. The very people he took in, loved, cared for, and trained were the very ones who were trying to destroy his credibility. Sadly, there were many Corinthians who bought in to the deception. His character was attacked.

They perverted the spiritual gifts. They winked at incest. They were abusive in their marriages. They were drunk at the Lord's table. They went to demon feasts. And their city was inundated with so many pagan beliefs that they were sorely confused. Meanwhile, Paul had traveled to Ephesus and things weren't going very well there either. It all culminated when a riot started that could have taken his life. Being a messenger of Christ was absolutely the greatest challenge he had ever faced.

Paul made this comment in 2 Corinthians 7:5:

> "For when we came into Macedonia, we had no rest, but we were harassed at every turn – conflicts on the outside, fears within."

Paul was battling with fear – afraid that all of his efforts at Corinth had come to naught. He had no rest, was troubled, agitated, and anxious. Here we find this marvelous man in the pit of despair over the disturbances of people in the church. Discouraged!

This is a dangerous place for leaders to find themselves. The seeming absence of God makes you feel all alone. Scripture reveals that Paul's spirit was restless and no joy was left in him. Every minister and church leader will, at times, experience the loss of joy. When you have invested your heart and soul into people, and yet everything you do seems to return with painful consequences, you can't help but be discouraged. There comes a sense of drudgery in the tasks of everyday life. Leaders are constantly seized with a feverish desire to go elsewhere – to resign and move on to greener pastures.

We may be tempted to give up on ministry, either as a volunteer or as a full time staff member, and find another occupation entirely. When you find yourself in this place it's easy to become bitter toward the church, jealous of other ministers, disgusted with our own lack of abilities, and disillusioned by hurtful words that have cut deep. This is what causes many to lose their spiritual and moral compass, drift out to sea, and abandon their call.

If you find yourself totally overwhelmed by discouragement, you're in good company with one of the greatest church planters the world has ever known.

Paul was on the edge, but he refused to quit.

> "We are hard pressed on every side, but not crushed; perplexed, but not in despair; persecuted, but not abandoned; struck down, but not destroyed." 2 Corinthians 4:8-9 (NIV)

Discouraged? Yes. But still holding on to hope.

Instead of looking down at the troubled sea and sinking, as Peter did, Paul lifted his eyes toward God in confidence, with a thankful heart.

At this time there were a lot of things he wasn't thankful for, such as the Christians who turned on him and left the church, all of the physical pain inflicted upon him, or the people who discredited his ministry. Those are painful and hurtful things. However, what Paul did next is what caused him to rise above.

> "But thanks be to God, who always leads us as captives in Christ's triumphal procession and uses us to spread the aroma of the knowledge of him everywhere." 2 Corinthians 2:14 (NIV)

Marching Behind the Commander-in-Chief

Let me give you a little background. Paul draws this encouragement from a very graphic historic event that occurred in his world. He uses that as a backdrop for what he says. He uses words like triumph, aroma, fragrance – all words that speak of a very unique happening of his time. The Romans had what was called a "Triumph." A Triumph was when the Roman government and all the people honored a great general or commander-in-chief who was returning from a victorious battle.

In the actual Triumph there would be a procession through the streets of Rome, concluding at the capital where an offering would be made to the gods. There would come the trumpeters, followed by a long parade of people and national dignitaries.

The honored general himself, wearing a purple robe embroidered with golden palm leaves, would follow, riding in a chariot pulled by four horses. In his hand he held an ivory scepter crowned with an eagle. As he passed through the crowds that lined the streets, people would throw flowers before the chariot in honor of their war hero. Horses would trample the flowers underneath their hoofs as they trotted down the streets of the city. A strong aroma from the flowers would fill the air, as the people would shout, "Triumph, triumph, triumph, triumph."

Now read Paul's words again. "But thanks be to God, who always leads us as captives in Christ's triumphal procession and uses us to spread the aroma of the knowledge of him everywhere."

That was the picture in Paul's mind. What a contrast it is from the pain he felt in his heart. He goes from the despair of being hurt and rejected by people to the exhilaration of being in a triumphal parade with his Commander-in-Chief, Jesus Christ. From a human viewpoint Paul looks like he's been defeated, not like a conquering hero. But when you turn your attention from the disappointments and difficulties of ministry to the triumphant calling and privileges of ministry, your perspective changes. Paul begins to give thanks.

He goes on to say, "But thanks be to God who always leads us." There is never a time, there is never a moment, and there is never an occasion when God is not leading.

> *There is never a time, there is never a moment, and there is never an occasion when God is not leading.*

We have the privilege of belonging to the ranks of the sovereign Lord; the privilege of marching behind the Commander-in-Chief as one of his lieutenants; the privilege of belonging to the victorious troops; the privilege of being under that kind of leadership – a leader who always leads to victory, who doesn't know defeat. We have the privilege of being chosen by God to be a soldier of Jesus Christ, to bear His name, to wear His uniform, and to serve His cause.

A thankful heart restored Paul's joy. If you find yourself in a difficult place, don't look at the circumstances. Don't focus on the difficulties or the people problems. If you want to turn your discouragement into joy, look at your privileges. Just contemplate the privilege of being counted in the ranks with the heroes of faith. WOW! What a privilege. To have been handpicked by the God of the universe. You enter into battle with a King who has never or who will never be defeated. You have purpose, everlasting purpose. Rejoice!

The church is the vehicle that changes the world, but the vehicle may not always look how we think it should look. I learned this great truth late in ministry. I so wish, as a young man, I would have had the spiritual wisdom that Paul exhibited, which I have learned over the years and now live by. What freedom and joy it has brought my family and me.

A Hot Smelly Ride

I pondered all of this as our family was driving to Amarillo, Texas to visit my mom. We had our three-year-old grandson, Asher, in the backseat. He's always more fun than a barrel of monkeys. As we were traveling down I-40, just west of Amarillo, there was a large stockyard. Every time we pass by, the smell is horrendous. That day it was 104 degrees outside and all that cow manure had been baking in the sun all day. The smell was almost unbearable. As I was driving I said, "Asher, what's that smell?" I looked in my rearview mirror at him sitting in his car seat and he was gagging. His eyes were red and teary. I laughed so hard I almost had to pull the car to the side of the road. Poor Asher! That was a horrible experience for the little guy. He was mad at me – like it was my fault. I think he was more upset because I couldn't stop laughing. As I continued driving into the outskirts of the city it made me think about the book I had just read to Asher a few nights before, Noah's ark, the great story found in Genesis chapter 6.

The ark was an Old Testament symbol of the church. The ark was the way of salvation, the plan to save the world. But the vehicle God designed to save them wasn't always pleasant. In fact, that yearlong boat ride, at times, was extremely troublesome, demanding, and just plain yucky. There were over 50,000 animals, seven people, a six hundred year old man, and in addition to all of that, provisions for a whole year.

As magnificent as this vehicle of safety was, it was also filled with an enormous amount of, I don't know how else to say it, animal crap! They stepped in it, slipped on it, fell in it and waded through mounds of crap. They shoveled it, tossed it, and pitched it out the windows. They didn't even know how to deal with all of the piles of it, but it didn't change the fact that this magnificent ship brought salvation to all who heeded the voice of God. The ark wasn't always comfortable and pleasant, but it was the way to salvation. I would venture to say the ark was a crappy experience much of the time.

It's an amazing picture of the New Testament church.

Be Careful Where You Step While In The House Of God

In the same way, the church is the vehicle of salvation. Through the church, millions of people around the world are saved. For all who enter in are offered the way to eternal life. But if you haven't noticed, the vehicle called the church is filled with a lot of dirty people, mean people, unpleasant people, lukewarm people, rude people, controlling people, abusive people, and just plain sinful people. In church you will experience a lot of crappy things because the church is in the "people business." Yet, it doesn't change the fact that this is the vehicle that leads the masses to salvation.

I've waded through more "church crap" than I've ever cared to, but what I have discovered is that the church is still the most beautiful thing I have ever witnessed.

I want to share something with you that is very personal. I was a young boy when I first realized my parents had a serious drug problem. They had an addiction that affected every member of our family. By being exposed to their addiction over a period of many years, I now suffer from the same drug addiction. Today, it has moved into another generation and I see the stronghold it has upon my children. Let me explain this life-altering drug addiction. My parents drug me to church on Sunday mornings, they drug me to church on Sunday nights, and they drug me to church every Wednesday night. They drug me to every revival and special church event. They had a serious drug problem. That church drug addiction is the very thing that developed a deep passion in me for God and His House.

This is a drug addiction for which I will be forever grateful. This addiction started when my parents brought me to church for the first time. I was just five days old and I've never been able to get it out of my system. My whole life has been shaped by the House of God. I gave my life to Christ in the church. I was baptized in the church. I memorized scriptures in the church. I found healing in the church. I was called to full-time ministry in the church. I met my wife in the church. We got married in the church. I've met lifelong friends in the church. My children were dedicated, received Christ as their Lord, and were baptized in the church. My kids discovered their lifelong callings in the church. My three boys have found their beautiful, godly wives in the church. The church has been the greatest gift I have ever received. There is no greater place on earth than the church. Don't ever forget the power of the church, even if you're knee deep in "church crap." Don't ever lose sight of the big picture. The sometimes-messy vehicle called the church is still the amazing, anointed, life-changing vessel that is moving millions of people heavenward year after year. And we get to be a part of the biggest rescue plan in the universe.

> *Don't ever forget the power of the church, even if you're knee deep in "church crap."*

Chapter 3

The C3 Miracle

The next few years were a battle of recovery. It was so amazing that despite all of the devastation, we never missed paying a bill or a salary check. Everyone, including myself, was sure that the closing of our church was inevitable. But that never happened.

Healing takes time but it always comes. We slowly climbed out of that dark hole to the place where we were no longer in danger of closing the doors. One year later we actually started slowly growing in numbers again. However, our growth always seemed to fall into a continuing cycle of growth and decline, growth and decline. It was like an invisible barrier that could not be breached. It certainly wasn't due to a lack of hard work. Our staff had given all they could, and yet nothing would work.

One particular day is forever imprinted on my mind. It began one Sunday morning. Standing in the front row of the auditorium, in the middle of worship, I looked over my shoulder at a very small crowd of people. We had recently gone to two services. This second service was certainly not out of need but more out of desperation – a need to do something different. That morning I could feel the sickening feeling sweeping over me again. It was the feeling that I was a failure as a pastor. It was all the same. We saw the same people week after week, same attendance year after year, and saw few salvations and few baptisms.

Worship was coming to an end and I was getting ready to step onto the stage to preach. I was so tired and all I could think of was how badly I wanted to step up there and resign. I was writing the letter in my mind. I can remember saying under my breath, "God, you mean this is all I was created for? I can't even fill a tiny little building like this?"

I was haunted by the thought that I had become a pastor to a dead, lifeless, declining church, which was the very thing I said I would never be. I felt like I didn't have the energy or desire to go on.

During that time we would sit in staff meetings and our youth pastor, Sean, would say, "Pastor, just tell us who we are as a church."

That was the most frustrating question I had ever been asked. I found myself struggling to find the answer. I would lay in bed at night with that question haunting me. I couldn't answer it. I couldn't figure it out. I didn't know who we were.

Living In Two Worlds

It was during this same time that Kay was the head of our worship department. She directed the choir and band and led worship as well. A few years before our decision to reach a young generation, we were trying desperately to be a little more progressive and up with the times. Instead of the staff sitting in those big throne chairs on stage, they were now sitting on the front row. The organ on our stage was a sacred relic from the past, very comparable to the Ark of the Covenant. We had gone through many different organists, and the way it was played always sounded like a funeral service. The first step to any form of progressive music was getting rid of it. The organ sat unused for months. One week I removed the organ bench. I'm not exaggerating the truth when I say that each week I slid the organ a few inches closer to the wall. A few months later it was up against the wall and remained there for over a year. One weekend it just vanished from our stage. I was the king of slow change in order to keep the peace at all cost. When Kay decided to remove the oversized grand piano with a golden engraved plaque stating who had donated it, the plan was for it to be replaced by a keyboard. This was sacrilege. The debates we had in our board meetings over that keyboard were ridiculous. The compromise we finally made was to purchase a keyboard but to put it in a baby grand piano casing. So, we went from a grand piano to a baby grand that was really a keyboard disguised as a piano so church people wouldn't be upset.

Kay was introducing new songs from Darlene Zschech of Hillsong Church. That was the new progressive church trend, and Kay was following their lead by adding more band members and singers. This style of music was very different from what most of our congregation was used to. I remember cringing when the songs were too loud or when an electric guitar lead was highlighted. With any new song Kay would introduce, half the congregation would cross their arms or sit down in protest against what they called "this new rock music." We quickly realized introducing contemporary worship into a traditional church can be a little like getting two cats into unity by tying their tails together and throwing them over a clothes line. After one Sunday morning service I was approached in the foyer by a longtime church member who was red in the face saying, "I've had it up to here with this music! I don't like it and that sound and beat make me violent!" I could clearly see that. He was a very unhappy Christian. Well, I'm not sure "Christian" is the right word. He was a very unhappy church person. Kay and I still joke about that to this day. We can be at a concert or in the middle of worship when it's rocking out and we will look at each other and say at the same time, "This music makes me violent!" It always causes us to laugh.

> *When church culture is unhealthy, everything becomes petty and we spend valuable time and energy on nonessentials.*

When church culture is unhealthy, everything becomes petty and we spend valuable time and energy on nonessentials.

Also, during that same time, we were trying to make cosmetic changes to our building. Our church had orange carpet and orange padded pews. We desperately wanted to change the pews with removable chairs to give us more flexibility and a more modern look.

The arguing and complaining over pews versus chairs was crazy. The topic was so sensitive that I had to take time out of the Sunday service to demonstrate how comfortable the chairs were. I had a chair on stage and invited one of the ladies, who was so upset over this pew decision, to come and try it out. I felt like a sales person: "See how beautiful and comfortable." They had extra back support, unlike our pews. They were removable and they linked together. "The kind of chair we want to purchase is called a Pew Chair." It was very important to get pew into that sentence. What I really wanted to say is, "Come on! Are you kidding me? Really? This is what we are going to spend our energy and time on? Have we forgotten that a million people die every week who are going to spend eternity somewhere? And here we are fighting over chairs, music, and pianos!"

With all of the changes we were making, the grumbling was growing intensely with the older crowd, while the younger crowd loved the new direction and wanted more. We were one church trying to live in two worlds. When people's personal preferences aren't catered to, that is when you will see their real inner person. And many times it's not pretty.

I think many church people are going to experience something very unpleasant when they reach what the Bible calls the Judgment Seat of Christ. This event takes place right after the Rapture of the Church. This is the moment all believers will stand one on one with Jesus Himself to be judged. Did our lives bring damage or benefit to God's Kingdom? Did we make His Kingdom about ourselves and our preferences? Or did we give that up so that many would come to know Him by our relating to them? Did we enhance the Kingdom by our generosity or hinder the Kingdom's advancement by our greed and stinginess? Did we live our lives producing the Fruit of the Spirit – love, joy, peace, etc. – or by the works of the flesh – discord, jealousy, fits of rage, selfish ambition, dissensions, and factions?

1 Corinthians 3:13-15 gives us another view of that moment:

> "Their work will be shown for what it is, because the Day will bring it to light. It will be revealed with fire, and the fire will test the quality of each person's work. If what has been built survives, the builder will receive a reward. If it is burned up, the builder will suffer loss but yet will be saved—even though only as one escaping through the flames."

This passage is talking about entering heaven with rewards or suffering loss. It's easy to point fingers at people who create dissension. But what about leaders who have been called to lead His church and yet allow man to stand in the way? As leaders we will stand at that same judgment and will be judged not only for how we have lived out our lives but also for how well we have led His people. Look at what James tells us:

> "Not many of you should become teachers, my fellow believers, because you know that we who teach will be judged more strictly." James 3:1 (NIV)

There is a more harsh judgment for leaders. That's why there is no room to allow for damaging forces. Whatever your level of leadership, lead strong and lead well!

By nature, I'm a peacemaker and mercy-driven with a "don't rock the boat" mentality. I just want everybody to be happy! But in reality, in this kind of divided environment, no one is fulfilled or happy. We were trying to live in two worlds, and neither was done well or with zeal. We were trying to be all things to all people. It was a constant struggle, attempting to make everybody happy. We couldn't afford making anyone mad because we feared they would leave the church.

One day, a staff member came to me and asked if our staff could go to C3. I didn't even know what a C3 was. He explained that it was a conference at a church in the Dallas area. At that point, the only thing that sounded good to me was getting out of town for a few days.

A small group of us traveled to Grapevine, Texas and drove up to a mammoth facility called Fellowship Church. The parking lot was packed and as we entered the front doors we were greeted by the friendliest people I'd ever encountered. You might even say that they were over the top. It was like Disneyland on steroids. We were ushered inside to a massive crowd that was buzzing. They were all so excited. I felt like they knew something I didn't know. You couldn't help but sense the excitement and anticipation. The doors opened and everyone started running to the front of the auditorium. We got caught up in the fast-moving crowd and found ourselves on the fourth row in the very center.

The service started, and it was completely different from anything I had ever experienced before. I sat in total amazement as Ed Young stepped out onto the stage – bigger than life. I held on to every word and I found myself not wanting his sermon to end. Church was electrifying, alive and engaging. For the first time ever, I experienced a production-style service. Lights, cameras, giant video screens and dancers. A huge curtain dropped and the worship team came out blazing. You felt like you needed to fasten your seat belt. This was church like never before!

My heart raced and my emotions became uncontrollable. Tears began to flow. I tried to stop them but I couldn't. I couldn't remember the last time I felt liberated in a church service. What I sensed was excitement and freedom. It was youthful and fun. It was like breathing fresh air.

After the service that evening our group went out to eat. I was so excited about what I had just experienced that I found myself inviting the waitress to attend Fellowship Church. I assured her she would love it! What I found so strange was that I couldn't remember the last time I'd invited someone to my own church. Why did I want to invite someone to this church?

Every session at the conference was just as exciting as the first. I had never seen anything on this scale. I didn't even know churches like this existed.

A few days later the conference was over – I wasn't ready for it to end. It left me hungry for more. We decided to catch the latest flight out that Saturday night so we could attend their Saturday afternoon service. We could not get enough. That Saturday morning I asked our staff to meet in my hotel room before checking out. I wanted to spend some time debriefing. I wanted to hear from each one what they had experienced. Going around the room each person expressed their thoughts about the conference. One by one, they shared. The room was filled with an air of excitement and hope. Their eyes were bright and conversation alive. It was like a light of hope had been switched on.

When everyone had finished, I stood, fighting back tears, and said, "Guys, I know who we are. I can finally tell you who we are. We are Fellowship Church." We had come to find out that Fellowship Church was one of the most cutting edge and creative churches in America and had a congregation of about twenty thousand people.

I can't tell you how foolish I felt saying that was who we were because we weren't anything like Fellowship Church. We weren't even a little bit like them. To state it correctly, we were as opposite from them as you could possibly be. Of course, I made that statement knowing you can't become someone else. It was what they were doing and how they were attracting and reaching a young generation that I found so appealing. For the first time in my life I saw it. I had experienced it. And I wanted it. It was a dream I could see and I wasn't about to let it go.

> *For the first time in my life I saw it. I had experienced it. And I wanted it.*

We traveled back home to our 75-year-old, traditional church. Our building was old and uninviting. We had duct tape holding down the seams of the carpet. On the inside we were religious and stuffy. Most everyone came to church wearing coats and ties. People were calling each other 'brother' and 'sister' instead of by their real names, which is a religious practice I have always disliked.

As I mingled through the crowd that Sunday morning, I had a smirk on my face. I felt I had a secret that no one else knew and I was about to explode.

The First Reveal, Ouch!!

That next week I called a board meeting to share with them what I had experienced at C3. I was prepared to share with them our new church vision. We all gathered in that small upstairs Sunday school room and I just blurted out that we are going to reach a young generation. I drew a target on the white board and boldly declared that we were going to be a church of all ages, focused on winning a young generation. I was standing in front of some great men and as I talked, they shook their heads in agreement. As I left, it sure seemed like all of our leadership had bought into this new direction...until the next morning. My secretary stepped into my office and said one of our board members wanted to see me, and that it was urgent.

She ushered him in and the moment I saw him I knew this wasn't going to be a good meeting. His face was as red as a beet. He was wearing a mean scowl and as he sat down he physically trembled with anger.

He started off by saying that the Holy Spirit woke him in the middle of the night to deliver me a message. He continued to express that the Holy Spirit was grieved by my promoting a vision that would focus on the young while excluding the senior adults of our church – those who had made this church what it is today and who bring the majority of the finances.

I assured him that he had misunderstood the vision. We who are mature are no longer going to focus on our own likes and desires. We're going to stop doing church in a way that is desirable to us. We are going to do church in a way that is attractive to a young generation which is moving further and further away from Christ.

He was so angry because I would not recant the vision that God had given me for our church. He proceeded to tell me that I was the worst preacher he had ever sat under. He said for him to be fed spiritually he had to attend a Presbyterian church down the street. In the course of that conversation he repeatedly stated how inadequate I was – making it crystal clear that I did not measure up as a pastor.

Just so we are all on the same page, if anyone claims to speak on behalf of God, and the conversation turns into a personal attack, it is not from God.

Isn't it odd how good people can be absolutely convinced that what God has put in motion is absolutely wrong and sinful?

After he walked out, I had a very difficult time dealing with his angry words. But for the first time in twelve years of pastoring, I didn't fold under the pressure. I didn't apologize. I didn't beg for him to stay. This was a person with a lot of clout. He had the ability to create a strong faction against me and the vision God had given me. But there was a calm deep inside of me. It was like an anchor keeping me steady. That anchor was the confidence of knowing who we were as a church. There was no doubt. No question. I had seen it. I had experienced it. God had confirmed it. And I was not wavering!

That day marked the beginning of a renewed sense of joy in pastoring. The same joy and excitement that I had as a twenty-three-year-old, ready to take on the world, was coming back. It's the power of knowing who you are and what God has called you to do.

Chapter 4

God, Help Me! I Don't Know What I'm Doing!

I was ready to take on the challenge but didn't have a clue where to start. I found myself exactly where I needed to be – admitting that my leadership and our church ministry were ineffective. As I sat in my office that morning I wrote out a long list of all the ministries in our church. I went methodically through each one, giving them a letter grade. When I had finished we were a C- church. It was clear to me why we were just maintaining – we were a little below average. To make things worse, the average church in America is at best maintaining, if not declining, and we were below that. It's a harsh reality to admit that the organization you've been leading for the past twelve years is struggling to stay afloat.

Our church had been a well established church of seventy-five years. There was a tremendous amount of tradition and ownership. How would I ever turn this ship in another direction? Most of the congregation thought everything was just fine and were very happy with *their* church just the way it was. But I knew that there was something far greater in store for all of us if we would be willing to challenge ourselves like the New Testament church.

Anxious to continue this adventure, I sat down early one morning at Starbucks with a pen and pad of paper. I wrote out several questions:

- Why is our church running at such a low level?
- Why have we been the same size for so many years?
- Why are we not winning hundreds and even thousands to Christ?
- Do I really believe the church is empowered by Christ himself?
- Do I believe the church is the most powerful institution on earth?

If the above was true, then the problem wasn't God, it was me! What was I doing wrong? It certainly wasn't a lack of hard work or desire. But clearly something wasn't right.

As I took a painful look at myself, desperately wanting to change, I began to realize that I was leading by a preconceived idea of how I thought church should function. That day, sitting in Starbucks, drinking an Americano with an extra shot of espresso, I was jolted into the reality that I was leading in the same way that had been modeled to me by the church in which I grew up. I was repeating what I had always seen and done in church.

This is why so many churches are caught in a time warp. It's the reason why so many churches are out of step and ineffective in reaching the people they say they are trying to reach. My mind began to drift toward my own family as an example. When I think about my role as a husband and father, I function largely by what was lived out in front of me as a kid. I'm primarily repeating what my dad did. By nature, we keep doing the same thing generation after generation. It's the easiest thing to do. It comes naturally to us and therefore it requires little or no effort on our part. That's why we often find ourselves repeating the actions of our parents. Even if we hated what they did, and declared we would never be like them, we often repeat the behaviors of molestation, alcoholism, and physical and sexual abuse. We repeat them because we've never taken the initiative in disciplining ourselves to live at a higher level.

Building A Lasting Legacy

Something I learned from my parents that made a tremendous impact upon my life was that we have the power to build off of each generation. My dad was an amazing Christian, husband, and father. I truly believe he lived life at his highest level. When

I was young he was constantly telling me that I was made to do great things. His desire was for me to surpass him at every level. When my father came to the end of his life, he had built a spiritual foundation for me to springboard into my future. His desire was for me to run faster and go higher and further than he had ever gone. He cheered me on to greatness every day.

As Kay and I raised our three boys, it was our desire to build off of the spiritual legacy of our parents. Not to ride on their coattails but to suit up like warriors on the front lines, advancing and taking new territory. Kay and I want to use our God-given talents to stretch us as far as possible. We want to give our boys that same foundation to springboard off of to run faster and go higher and further for the Kingdom of God than we ever dreamed. Family members need to declare together that there cannot be a weak link in their family line. We cannot afford for any family member to rebel and walk away from God's plan. Every family member needs to understand that their mission is to go higher than the previous generation. This is how we change the world – one child at a time and one generation at a time. But if we choose to skate through life, enjoying what has been given to us without personal investment, we will not advance from the former generation.

This is a great illustration of what has happened to the American church. We've been riding on the coattails of church leadership for the past thirty, forty, and fifty years. It seems church leadership is stuck in the past. We've lost our creativity. We've lost the boldness to be reformers. We've lost the desire to rock the boat and make the necessary changes to reach a changing society. Many of our churches today still look like they did twenty years ago, yet we all agree we live in a different world than we did twenty years ago.

No one in their right mind would believe the way we ministered to people in the sixties would be the most effective way to minister to people today. And yet that's exactly what's happening. We're just repeating what we have seen and experienced. It's a religious rut we often find ourselves in, and any other practice that isn't common or comfortable seems foreign and wrong. It's been said that a rut is nothing but a grave with both ends kicked out. To a large degree, the American church has fallen in the death-rut and can't get out.

> *"What, then, is the true Gospel of consistency? Change!"*

It causes us to be completely out of touch with the outside world that we are supposed to be reaching. Mark Twain once said, "What, then, is the true Gospel of consistency? Change!"

That statement is so true, but seems to be the opposite of how most people live out their lives. The one consistent thing in our lives as leaders must be change.

I definitely knew I had worn a deep groove in a ministry style and I was stuck in a rut. The definition of that phrase, "stuck in a rut," means being caught in a boring lifestyle that never changes.

That described my situation perfectly.

That night I invited some key staff members to our home. As we sat around I asked them the same questions that I had pondered earlier that morning. What would draw a young, unchurched generation back to church? What are we doing that has distanced ourselves from them? Who are they? What do they need? What is their view of the church? I threw it out on the table for the discussion to begin. I was looking forward to a deep theological debate about church growth. I was sorely disappointed in the direction of the conversation.

My son Dustin had just graduated from a Bible college, and we had just brought him on to our staff as our student ministries pastor. He spoke up and told me that if I would get rid of that big ugly pulpit on stage and start wearing jeans and in-style shirts, we would start growing. I couldn't help it – I laughed out loud. I said, "Dustin, I don't mean to offend you, but that's ridiculous! Your idea of reaching the lost is removing the pulpit and wearing jeans?" He leaned forward in his chair and said, "Dad, we are not relating to our culture. We live in Albuquerque. No one dresses up in our city except stuffy preachers and lawyers." It ignited a lively conversation that all seemed directed at me.

Like I'm out of touch, or even worse, out of style. Someone blurted out, "You need to dress like Ed Young." Another said, "You need to preach like him too." "You need to fix your hair differently." "You need to lose weight." I could feel myself getting defensive. I reminded myself that all these comments were coming from young staff members. It's just the voice of immaturity. How shallow! I could feel my deep-rooted, religious ideas taking hold. Digging in deep, not wanting to change, I found myself rejecting this foolishness – fighting against the very vision I had put into motion. Change is always more difficult when it affects you personally. I found myself frustrated with all this frivolous talk. After everyone had gone home, I must admit that the meeting left me more confused and frustrated than when we had started.

> *Change is always more difficult when it affects you personally.*

Later that evening my wife Kay said, "You know they are right. You need to listen to them. They are the very age of those we are trying to reach."

I didn't sleep much that night. I realized there was a great chasm between my religious ideas and a young generation that knows nothing about God. That night it became crystal clear to me that we were embarking on a major paradigm shift that was going to radically affect everyone in our church. It was at this point I knew we couldn't afford to be wrong. This couldn't be about following a new church fad or someone's crazy idea of what they think church is supposed to be. There are so many opinions of how to do church. Who's right and who's wrong?

It was later that week that I made a point to get up much earlier than usual to start reading through the books of Acts and Corinthians. I desperately wanted to know why the New Testament church was so effective in reaching the lost. As I followed the missionary travels of the apostle Paul, I saw that he too was entering into cultures that were very different from his own. He learned to be incredibly strategic in how to lead masses of people to the Lord. Look at his strategy:

> "Even though I am free of the demands and expectations of everyone, I have voluntarily become a servant to any and all in order to reach a wide range of people: religious, nonreligious, meticulous moralists, loose-living immoralists, the defeated, the demoralized—whoever. I didn't take on their way of life. I kept my bearings in Christ—but I entered their world and tried to experience things from their point of view. I've become just about every sort of servant there is in my attempts to lead those I meet into a God-saved life. I did all this because of the Message. I didn't just want to talk about it; I wanted to be in on it!" 1 Corinthians 9:19 (MSG)

This passage became the cornerstone of our transition from an old, traditional church, with our focus on church people, to a relevant, missional church focusing on the unchurched.

This passage lay open on my desk for weeks. I was pondering the apostle's words – the wisdom of the greatest church planter the world has ever known. He stayed very focused on what the mission of the church was: make disciples and reproduce. I found myself analyzing every word. He says, "Even though I am free of the demands and expectations of everyone…"

Legalism.

What does he mean by this? Paul was a devout Jew with religious traditions that had been bred into his culture for hundreds of years. Their religious culture was very exclusive and they truly believed they were superior over other nationalities and cultures. Everything was based on works. They were always concerned about how they measured up in the eyes of their fellow Jewish brothers and sisters. It had become a very self-centered and self-serving religion. They were overly concerned with their outward appearances and the approval of their peers. This is why Jesus said, "Woe to you, scribes and Pharisees, hypocrites! For you cleanse the outside of the cup and dish, but inside they are full of extortion and self-indulgence."

Jesus scolded them for putting on an outward facade while they were inwardly filled with corruption. It was only after Paul's dramatic conversion on the road to Damascus that his eyes were opened to a new reality. He was no longer bound by the expectations of religious rituals and the traditions of man. This is the trap of legalism.

Legalism is still very much alive in our culture.

Let me give you an example of this today. In the extreme religious, conservative movements, there are demands and expectations placed upon women regarding how they look and dress. Women are taught not to cut their hair, not to wear pants, not to wear makeup, not to dress stylishly, not to adorn themselves with jewelry. They are taught to look as plain and drab as possible because we must come out and be separate from the world. It's taught as an act of holiness. Yet in this same movement the men dress stylishly, have up-to-date haircuts, and are clean-shaven. On the street you could not identify them from anyone else. Why the double standard? And why is it that women are placed under this kind of pressure to look a certain way outwardly? The reason why she will not wear modest pants to church on a freezing cold day or cut and color her hair to improve her appearance has nothing to do with holiness. It's because of what people will say. It is due to the fear of coming under condemnation and the scrutiny of fellow believers in her church. The women know they will be looked down upon or scorned and maybe even rejected. These Christians have been conditioned to believe this is a higher spiritual standard of holiness. Who told them that? Who started that train of thought and tradition? A hundred years ago it was someone's personal conviction and now, through several generations, it has been misconstrued into a Biblical truth. And people live it out as one of the highest spiritual standards in their lives.

Paul said he was free from all of that junk! (The laws of man)

This is why Jesus said to the Pharisees that they put heavy yokes upon the people and do not lift a finger to help them. This is the very thing that Christ came to free people from.

> *We were not saved to live up to the standards of man but only the standard of God's Word.*

We were not saved to live up to the standards of man but only the standard of God's Word.

People are sickened by churches today because we still get caught up in outward appearances. Yesterday I read a Facebook post from a pastor talking about his new member's class. He went on to say that a part of their class is dedicated to teaching those in attendance how to dress for church. He said, "There are school clothes and there are work clothes, and therefore, there are church clothes. We expect you to look a certain way. As a member, you are to have no tattoos or body piercings." When I read it I thought, "You've got to be kidding!"

Is that really what we want to emphasize? When we follow this train of thought, what are we saying to the world?

When Jesus was confronted by the Pharisees and the adulterous woman, look at what He focused on:

> "Hearing that, they walked away, one after another, beginning with the oldest. The woman was left alone. Jesus stood up and spoke to her. 'Woman, where are they? Does no one condemn you?' 'No one, Master.' 'Neither do I,' said Jesus. 'Go on your way. From now on, don't sin.'" John 8:10-11 (MSG)

Jesus didn't have outward religious expectations, but internal. Salvation was an issue of the heart.

This is exactly what Paul was saying, that he was now free of the expectations of others and no longer bound by their expectations.

———•———

I had just returned from Mombasa, Kenya. Our church had taken on a ten-year commitment to an unreached people group, the Digo tribe. An estimated 98 percent of Digo are Muslim. The women walk around in one hundred degree weather wearing a black hijab, five layers of clothing, with their heads and faces completely covered. Muslim men and women are both required to dedicate themselves to 'god,' but it is only women who are expected to demonstrate this dedication outwardly in the form of a hijab. Why women and not men? The Muslim women are conditioned to believe it's a spiritual act, but actually it was established by Muhammad out of his own insecurity. As a husband of many wives, he needed to come up with a way to control them.

This is the history of the hijab. Muhammad had a large number of wives, most of them young and beautiful, some even younger than his grandkids. Once, he heard some of his followers talking about how many beautiful young wives he had. They were surprised by the large age difference between them. A young follower of his said that if he had the chance, he would marry Muhammad's child-wife Aisha after the Prophet's death. So, Muhammad sought ways to prevent others from desiring his wives. He ordered his wives to wear veils and not show their face or any part of their body to other men. He knew that if people did not see his wives, they would never know their age and their beauty. It was a selfish, evil act of control. Now, hundreds of years later, women are forced into this bondage, and yet they believe it's pleasing to God.

Islam prescribes women to start wearing the hijab at the age of 6. It was likely ordered by Muhammad since he married his wife Aisha at the age of six. If Muhammad had married Aisha or another girl at the age of three, he more than likely would have ordered women to wear the hijab from the age of three. He made this law out of his greed and lust for many women. Now, today, millions of women are bound by the expectations of a man-made law and sadly believe it's pleasing to God.

On the Judgment Day, God will never ask women if they wore the hijab or scarf, Indian sari or Western dress, dirty clothes or clean clothes, pants or a dress. This kind of mentality leads to hypocrisy. It's not about outward appearances that project a spiritual persona. It's about purity of the heart.

Jesus addresses this very thing with the religious of his day:

> "And when you pray, do not be like the hypocrites, for they love to pray standing in the synagogues and on the street corners to be seen by others. Truly I tell you, they have received their reward in full." Matthew 6:5 (NIV)

Growing up in the church, I found that there was an abundance of what I call "Facade Christians." As an example, there were those who believed that the movie theater was a sinful place. They wouldn't set foot into a theater. If that's someone's personal conviction, it should never be condemned. The problem is when they force their expectations on other people as if it lifts them to a higher level of spirituality. When it comes to the movie industry, I'm personally alarmed by the negative impact that many movie producers are having on society. But at the same time there are a lot of great and entertaining movies that I enjoy watching with my family. Now this is where outward appearances become hypocritical. Some Christians, who don't believe in going to a movie theater and openly declare it as worldly and sinful, will go to a Red Box and rent movies and watch every PG-13 and R-rated movie that comes out. That's the kind of action that caused Jesus to call the Pharisees hypocrites – declaring something publicly, to be seen in a spiritual act, but not living it in the privacy of their own homes.

We can look at these examples with a critical eye, but in reality we all fight the very same thing: the traditions of man. We naturally gravitate toward, and place more attention on, public performance rather than the inner transformation of the heart. These are two very different things.

I'm A Good Christian Boy

Let me explain it like this:

I grew up in church and in a good, godly home. My mother had a tremendous impact upon my life and is one of the greatest women of our day. She taught me to be a good Christian boy; to always be on my best behavior; to be polite, smile, say yes ma'am and no ma'am and to respect my elders. I had it down! I knew how to behave. The problem with this is that the Bible doesn't teach us to try to behave, it teaches of an inner work called the transformation of the heart. It's Christ working in you, and when it works its way out it's called the Fruit of the Spirit. Christ changes our behavior, but behavior never changes the heart. You can be on your best behavior at school, at home, or at work, yet on the inside lust, greed, and jealousy eat away at you like a cancer. No matter how good you look and how polished you are on the outside, that which is on the inside will constantly haunt us and periodically will burst out publicly. At times we will wonder, "Where did that come from? Why did I say that? Why am I so filled with thoughts of lust or so frustrated and angry all the time?" We ask, "What's wrong with me? What's up with that?"

> *Christ changes our behavior, but behavior never changes the heart.*

The problem is usually that the focus of our Christianity has been placed on looking good and behaving well in front of others instead of focusing on Christ's work in us. This was highly confusing to me as a high school kid. I did my best to be a good person and live up to others' expectations. But it always seemed like something was missing. Week after week at the end of the pastor's message, I would be so convicted that I would get up out of my seat and respond to the altar call, receiving Christ all over again. I've been saved more times than anybody I know. The mistake I made was focusing on behavior instead of Christ. I look back now and see that I was trying to live the Christian life by public performance and the approval of others, and was totally unaware of it.

When Paul was transformed by Jesus Christ, it must have been like a heavy weight was removed from his shoulders. Paul had been caught in tradition and had been controlled by the opinion of others for too long. Now he had only one to follow and one to impress.

Time was slipping away quickly that morning and I needed to get to the office but I found myself so captivated by Paul's words I could not pull myself away. I continued to read:

> "....I have voluntarily become a servant to any and all in order to reach a wide range of people: religious, nonreligious, meticulous moralists, loose-living immoralists, the defeated, the demoralized—whoever." 1 Corinthians 9:19 (MSG)

Zeroing In On The Lost

Another question I asked myself was, "Am I a servant to the non-religious?" I kept asking that question. I had to admit to myself that I wasn't. I was a servant to church people. I didn't even know any non-religious people. How did that ever happen? Christ made it very clear that He did not come for the healthy but came for the sick.

For much of Paul's life he had personally experienced the horrifying sickness of sin. He knew all too well of the debilitating destruction of this sickness. He was satanically driven to brutally murder Christians – hunting them down like animals. That's why he had an uncanny vision of the purpose of the Church – zeroing in on the loose-living immoralists, the defeated, the demoralized, and whoever crossed his path. He had walked in their shoes and now he wanted them to walk in his. They needed the same thing he had found. They became the focus of his message.

As I read these words over and over it became clear to me that our church was one-sided. Unlike Paul, who hung out with a wide range of lost people, I was hanging out with a narrow range of Christian people. I was hanging out with church people, and our church people were hanging out with other church people. We had found ourselves isolated from those who were desperately in need of Christ and His Church.

As I continued to research, I found that at the time the average person comes to Christ they are closely associated with twenty unchurched people. But the alarming trend is that the longer we follow Christ, the less associations we have with the unchurched. That means the more mature we grow, and the longer we serve Christ and His church, the less influence and impact we have with those far from God. Does that make any sense? It seems completely backward from the New Testament model.

My entire ministry had revolved around church people and somehow I had justified that way of thinking for the past fourteen years of pastorate.

There seems to be a big debate today on the purpose of the church and for whom it exists. Do we cater to the saved or to the unsaved? Do we design our worship service to attract Christians or non-Christians? If our answer is that all of this is for Christians, that means that Jesus Christ came for "Church People." Have we completely ignored the most famous verses in the Bible?

> "For God so loved the world that he gave his one and only Son..." John 3:16 (NIV)

> "Go into all the world and preach the good news to all creation." Mark 16:15 (NIV)

Jesus came for the world.

Do we design the church for what Christians want or for what non-believers need?

———◆———

This debate has been going on for the past two thousand years. Paul found himself in the city of Ephesus having to deal with the religious (church people) and the true role of the church:

> "Paul entered the synagogue and spoke boldly there for three months, arguing persuasively about the kingdom of God." Acts 19:8 (NIV)

He went into the synagogue. This was the place where church W ГШ! people hung out. They were religious people. They had memorized the first five books of the Old Testament. They were experts on prophecy. Every day they were looking for the signs of the coming Messiah.

They were prideful in their intellectual knowledge of God's word. They had an attitude of superiority and were prejudiced against anyone outside of their belief system. They had completely embraced the mindset: Us four and no more. Paul spent three long months trying to open their eyes to the purpose of the Kingdom of God. There are only two thoughts regarding the Kingdom: Either we are going to believe the Kingdom of God is for me and about me, or we believe the Kingdom of God is about loving, reaching, attracting, and designing everything for people disconnected from God. They debated it for three long months:

> "But some of them became obstinate; they refused
> to believe and publicly maligned the Way." Acts 19:8
> (NIV)

Can you even imagine religious people being obstinate? And furthermore, it says they maligned the Way. Maligned means to have an evil intent. There was something happening below the veneer of human flesh. Spiritual warfare was raging. God was working through his servant Paul, and Satan was working through religious, stiff-necked people. Satan always works the same strategy within the church. He deceives us into believing it's for me and about me.

The religious will always gravitate to exclusiveness and create an environment that is comfortable and safe. That concept is evil, but we're deceived into believing it's right. The Jews did not want the sinners, the Samaritans, or the barbaric Romans coming in and ruining what they had worked so hard to develop. Even more than that, they didn't want outsiders, who they considered defiled and tainted, to come in and ruin their reputation.

Outsiders would upset the applecart of hundreds of years of Jewish traditions.

What Paul was confronted with was an evil that flowed out of their religious traditions that resulted in having no tolerance for outsiders.

After three months Paul decided to walk away from their religious culture – a belief system based on following Jehovah God, yet stood against everything for which Christ came and died.

Paul's decision to walk away from a legalistic, stale church culture was the monumental moment when the church exploded in growth across the known world.

———◆———

Quickly another hour had passed and I was still sitting in that same spot in Starbucks. My mind was drifting to so many experiences I have had that were so similar to what Paul dealt with. Human nature never changes. The church today is still fighting the same religious mindset that was so destructive in Paul's day. It cannot be allowed to reign within the church any longer.

The Pharisaic voice is always loud and sounds so spiritual on the surface, but underneath it is prideful and arrogant. They want nothing to do with the ungodly, and they would never admit it, but they don't want them coming into the church until they act and look like church people. The view is that "those people" don't fit into their social community. "Those people" will negatively influence their kids. "Those people" are not their kind of people.

This is a controlling spirit that is extremely common in long-time, established churches and damages the expansion of the Kingdom of God.

That morning, as I stared out the window, I had a mental picture that actually caused me to laugh out loud.

It was Easter Sunday morning and as I walked out my front door it was a gorgeous sunny day. We had an amazing day planned, a musical production called The Messiah, and we were expecting a capacity crowd. All the way to church that morning I was praying for the many people who would attend that did not know Christ. I was praying that this might be their day of salvation. As I drove behind the church to park, some of the cast members were already in costume and they had gathered in the back for a cigarette break. As I parked, I said to myself, "Well, there they are, the smoking disciples." We had recruited a ragtag group of guys to be the twelve disciples. Some of these guys had lived rough lives, and I'm not so sure all of them had even made a commitment to Christ. But they loved attending church and being a part of this Easter production.

So, I'm out there slapping them on their backs and laughing and telling jokes, when at that very moment one of the most persnickety old ladies I've ever met walked up. She was a long-time member and had been a thorn in my side for years. Nothing was ever right. She had something negative to say about everything I did and every decision I made. On this sacred Easter Sunday morning, as she walked in my direction, she viewed her pastor hanging out in the back of the church with a rough crowd who were all sucking on their cigarettes...and probably hearing a few choice words as well. At that moment, I knew this was going to be an Easter greeting I would never forget.

As she walked toward me all I could think of was how she reminded me of the mean old woman in the Wizard of Oz who took Dorothy's little dog and crammed it in the basket on the bicycle. That was one scary woman! Remember, she was the wicked witch in Dorothy's dream. As she was approaching, that was the first thing I thought, "Here comes the Wicked Witch of the West." I reached over and opened the door for her and politely said, "Good morning." As I followed her inside, she spewed like a volcano.

"That is the most disturbing scene I have ever witnessed. Men dressed as disciples of Christ smoking on church property. I am so upset that it has made me physically ill. This has ruined my Easter. This is a disgrace and I'm grieved in my spirit. You need to go back out there and put a stop to that smoking right now!" As we came to a split in the hallway she was going one way and I was going the other way. I said, "Well I would rather hang out with smoking disciples than old, negative, gossiping church people." Then, I walked very quickly to my office. That was not a happy Easter for her, but it was a great day for all who attended the services. The smoking disciples were amazing that morning, and many people came to know Christ that day.

Today's "church culture" is killing the American church. This kind of thinking permeates churches across our nation. It is why 85 percent of churches have plateaued or are declining in numbers. Five thousand churches close their doors every year. Christian America is slowly coming to the understanding that we have grossly missed the mark.

Paul knew in his day that the mentality of the religious was way off track. The people were resistant to change, desperately wanting to hold onto their traditions and style, so Paul left them. He went into downtown Ephesus and rented out the lecture hall. He started teaching a small group of people about Christ and their calling to change the world. To accomplish this, Paul had to walk away from an old church culture of self-centeredness and start a new church culture that was centered on others. This is amazing! They took the Word of God out of the church and took it to the streets. Within two years, scripture tells us, *all* had heard the message of Christ. All? Everyone in the entire province? Within two years they had touched a half-million people with the message of Christ. They did it with no cell phones, Facebook, printed materials, TV, or billboards.

They just loved Jesus so much that they demonstrated His love and told other people about Him. Paul established the most important principle in church growth. He saw himself as a servant to everyone with whom he crossed paths. In other words, he was a laborer for the Kingdom of God.

After reading these words, I leaned back in my chair and thought, we've made church too difficult, too complicated. If we would just come back to the two most important commands that Jesus spoke. First was to love God and second was to love people. Just do what Jesus did. As church leaders, we are not here to be served and catered to, but to serve others.

I had become so intrigued, that I could not stop reading.

Paul continues:

> "I didn't take on their way of life. I kept my bearings in Christ— but I entered their world and tried to experience things from their point of view."

Live A Little In The Real World

What stood out to me about what Paul said was that he took the initiative to enter their world. The world he entered was full of hurt, poverty, sickness, hopelessness, and hostility. He was willing to meet them where they were.

Have you really ever thought about why Jesus was born in a manger? It was a place fit only for animals. It was a place of filth, dirt, dust, and straw, mixed with animal discharge. You can't get any lower than that. He didn't choose to be born among royalty. He chose to enter our world and experience it from the lowest levels of humanity. He didn't isolate himself in a palace or temple, surrounded by wealth. He walked among humanity experiencing poverty, rejection, persecution, and even murder. The reason he did this is because we can't win the masses until we are willing to enter their world. In other words, quit catering to the saved week after week and focus on the people who are tragically bound for hell.

By and large, church people enter the world of other believers while avoiding those who are anti-God or anti-church. For most Christians, entering "their" world is too risky and uncomfortable. Instead, we gravitate to our fellow believers where it's relaxing and enjoyable. Entering the world of the lost is hard work. Maybe that's why Jesus said, "The harvest truly is great, but the laborers are few; therefore pray the Lord of the harvest to send out laborers into His harvest." Luke 10:2 (NKJV)

This verse really piqued my interest. How do we create a church of laborers who are willing to enter the world of the unchurched and learn what makes them tick? What is their view of Christianity and the Church? What are their needs? What do they like to do? Where do they hang out and why?

Paul strategically entered into the lives of people far away from God for one reason, that he might introduce them to Christ, befriending them, walking with them, and learning to do life with them. Paul is clearly spelling out the lifestyle of the New Testament church. This is where we have failed as the American church. Over the past fifty years we have developed a church culture of isolation. So many churches are tightly knit together and they've created little church huddles. It's just like watching a football team huddling tightly together, arm in arm on the football field. If you're not in the huddle, all you see is a bunch of big butts. When the world looks in the direction of the church, that's all they see – a bunch of isolated butts. I did not want to admit it, but we as a church were more concerned about our church happiness than serving the lost. The thought so gripped me that a prayer of agony slipped out of my mouth: "Dear God, please don't let me be a 'butt' to the world anymore! I don't want to exclude them, but include them."

Paul's vision of the church was anything but isolation. He intentionally went after them. His three different trips of evangelism and church planting are referred to as his three missionary journeys. This is exactly the mentality we must have to impact our world for Christ.

We Do It There, But Not Here

My brother Steve and his family were missionaries on a foreign field for sixteen years. I'll never forget the day they left with three small children. They were leaving everything behind, which included most of their belongings, friends, and family. It was a heart-wrenching day. Before leaving, they went through a five-week missionary boot camp. They were taught "contextualization."

Contextualization teaches how to have the greatest impact on a foreign culture. You must fit in and identify with the culture before you can impact that culture. It means you have to change your clothing style, your customs, what you eat, and even your language. You have to change everything that is common to you and everything that is comfortable. You choose to disrupt your normal life for one reason: to reach people far from God. By and large, the American church is resistant to the idea of adapting ministry in a way a young generation can relate. We are not willing to disrupt our lives for someone else and not willing to change our religious customs and traditions to accomplish the very thing for which Christ died – saving lost people.

We applaud contextualization on the mission field and we applaud the missionary who changes everything to win the lost. We resist contextualization in our own churches because now it affects us!

I hear people say that most churches don't change and advance because of fear. That's not true. It's out of selfishness. If we change, it will disrupt the church culture that we enjoy and with which we are comfortable – feeling satisfied with our lives – content that we will spend eternity in heaven.

> *If we change, it will disrupt the church culture that we enjoy and with which we are comfortable*

I glanced down again at my Bible and read this last verse:

> "I've become just about every sort of servant there is in my attempts to lead those I meet, into a God-saved life. I did all this, because of the Message. I didn't just want to talk about it; I wanted to be in on it!"

What Do Church People Look Like?

Paul was willing to do whatever it took to relate to the unsaved. In the passage of 1 Corinthians 6, Paul describes the spiritual and moral climate of that city: sexually immoral, idolaters, adulterers, male prostitutes, homosexuals, thieves, greedy, drunkards, slanderers, and swindlers.

The apostle Paul was preaching to these people. They were the people who made up the church. Paul's writings left me with a burning on the inside to make my life count for the Kingdom of God. Was I created for smallness or greatness? I wanted to say greatness but I'm not sure I even believed in myself or in my leadership. Most of all, I wondered whether I was setting myself up for another church split. "Dear God, I can't go through that again!"

That entire week I spent much of my time away from people, trying to find direction for the future. At the end of the week, I was confronted with the decision.

Do we rock the boat and go for it, or not? Then I was hit with the real question, "What has God called me to do?" And I knew it was to win the lost at all costs! I stood up that morning, after reading the above passage from the apostle Paul, asking myself, "If need be, am I willing to walk away from a stale, religious culture even at the cost of upsetting many people who believe the church is 'just fine' as it is?" That morning I declared, no matter what, I will never back down…EVER AGAIN!

Chapter 5

Is There Just One "Caleb" in the House?

After 14 years of mediocre results in ministry, I think I was just sick and tired of being sick and tired. My life was passing me by ever so quickly and I was willing to put everything on the line. I needed to do something that moved us in this new direction. I called our staff together late one Friday night. We decided that the first step to take in creating a production-style service would be to paint the back wall of the auditorium stage black, to put up white spandex triangles and to add a few colored lights.

Up to this time our stage had been very traditional and formal. The stage background was a faux finished light purple with tall white columns and arches across the top. My thought was, "If larger churches have a black stage wall, then we are going to have a black wall to move us in that direction." One of the hardest things I've ever done was to roll the first stripe of black across that sacred purple paint.

It was our first step in saying, "We are willing to change in order to reach a younger generation." That Saturday morning when a church member stopped by and saw the black wall, you would have thought we had invited demons into our church. The moment he saw it he blurted out, "With all that black paint it makes our church look like a satanic church." That was definitely not the response I was hoping for. In light of his warm and affirmative reaction, I was preparing for a major backlash that Sunday morning. To my surprise, when the service started and our eight cheap production lights hit the stretched spandex, the stage came alive. And for the most part, people grinned and bore it.

On this journey, I found that as I preached about winning those who are far away from God, people would nod their heads in approval and shake my hand on the way out the door saying, "Pastor, great message this morning. You're right, Pastor! This young generation needs God."

Every Sunday morning I took the opportunity to cast the vision. I explained why I believe that in every church the young generation should be the overriding focus. I used all kinds of statistics to show them why this was so important. I shared with them that 19 out of 20 Christian people become Christians before they reach the age of 24. After the age of 25, 1 in 10,000 come to Christ. After age 35, 1 in 40,000. After 55, 1 in 300,000. After 65, 1 in 500,000. And after 74, 1 in 700,000 people.

If we want to make a spiritual impact in this world, then we have to reach out to the young. Their hearts and minds are still open and they are still searching for truth – yet the church is not speaking their language. I shared with them the frightening trends regarding the direction our nation is headed spiritually.

In America, only 12 percent of people under 18 regularly attend church. That means a stunning 88 percent of America's teenagers are unchurched. By current trends, out of all the children born in the last five years only 4 percent will serve Christ as adults.

Out of 7 billion people on earth, 4 billion are under 20 years of age. The majority of our world is made up of kids. Spiritually, we are losing this generation. Someone needs to sound the alarm and wake up the church. I think the most shocking thing of all is that the church of America, by and large, is still "doing" church for the older generation. These are people who have been in church for the past thirty to fifty years.

And we justify it because everyone knows that if you change things – if you disrupt the routine of the long-time attendees – church people will leave the church. You can't afford to make church people mad, as they are the ones who finance the church. So, church leaders are frozen by fear and keep doing the same things they have always done, even if it's ineffective in achieving

God's Kingdom agenda. This is the exact place I found myself. The last thing I wanted to do was lose the older population of our church.

We had worked very hard on building a senior adult ministry. Every month it grew in numbers. It was very exciting. They were now having sixty to seventy senior adults show up for their monthly meetings. They were in a season of life where they had time to invest into the ministry. Each month we were presenting them with ministry opportunities to invest into the lives of others. Ministries such as visitation teams, prayer teams, greeting, ushering, outreach, and community service. Unfortunately, few were interested in serving. It was like pulling teeth trying to get them to volunteer for anything.

What I started noticing was a disturbing trend. After every monthly meeting the leader of this ministry would come to me to tell me about all of their complaints. One of their main complaints was that I wasn't doing enough home visits. Also, if I didn't show up at the hospital to pray for them before a surgery, in their minds, I had failed my obligation to them as a pastor. Do you know how many surgeries that age group has?!

It was like they were keeping record of who I visited and who I didn't. If one of them was going into the hospital, thirty of their friends from the church would show up in the waiting room for support. They didn't see that as the powerful support structure of the church with believers ministering to one another. In their eyes, the church succeeded or failed depending on whether I showed up or not. A sick person in the hospital could have been visited by ten different people from the church and yet complain the entire time that no one from the church came to visit them. What they really meant was that the pastor didn't show up.

They were highly offended if I sent another staff member. They would say things like, "He sent a junior pastor instead of coming himself." Somehow they had developed the mentality that if I showed up at the hospital and prayed for them, it validated their worth in our church. I began to realize this group of 50 to 70-year-olds had an improper view of the church. Most of them had been raised in small churches that catered to church people instead of mobilizing them for ministry. Many churches hire a pastor to meet their needs. If he doesn't properly fulfill that duty, they vote him out and find one who will. This mentality is the complete opposite of the Biblical model. The reason why there are so many church conflicts is because people have misunderstood the Biblical concept of the responsibility of body of Christ. Paul explained this very principle:

> "So Christ himself gave the apostles, the prophets, the evangelists, the pastors and teachers, to equip his people for works of service, so that the body of Christ may be built up." Ephesians 4:11-12 (NIV)

The One Another Concept

Through leadership and organization the church becomes a powerful ministry machine. The pastor merely organizes the church body to love and minister to one another – equipping the saints for the work of the ministry.

It's interesting when you do a Google search on the "one anothers" in scripture. Fifty-nine are listed, and it's extremely clear how this becomes the strength of the church. Everyone is ministering to "one another." We are all servants just as Jesus came not to be served but to serve – our senior adult group was struggling with this concept. The attitude was, "I deserve the head pastor's attention and if I don't get it, he's going to hear about it." This was a good group of people, but something was missing. Being around them always put me on edge. You could sense a judgmental and critical spirit. A handful of them were just plain mean with their verbal assaults. I often thought, "I've never been talked to like this, even by non-Christians." I seriously tried to understand and make sense out of why so many church people are so demanding and unpleasant to be around.

When Christ enters our lives, something dramatic happens. We are now driven by a spirit of love. Paul said this:

> "For the entire law is fulfilled in keeping this one command: 'Love your neighbor as yourself.'" Galatians 5:14 (NIV)

That's the standard for every believer. Paul goes on:

> "But the fruit of the Spirit is love, joy, peace, forbearance, kindness, goodness, faithfulness, gentleness and self-control." Galatians 5:22-23 (NIV)

Sit, Soak and Sour

Let me ask you a question. Do you know of people who are longtime, faithful church attendees who are critical and hateful? The fruit of the spirit is not evident in them. They are people who have been Christians for many years and who seem to find the bad in everything. I've given this much thought and this is what I've come to believe: The Word of God has literally rotted inside of them. They have been sitting in church for thirty, forty, and fifty years and have made their Christian experience all about church attendance. They sit, soak, and sour. For years they sit in a pew and soak in the Word of God. Over a period of time, they sour on God's Word. It's when religion overrides transformation and it becomes a pharisaic spirit. The Word of God rots on the inside of them because it wasn't intended for us to hoard and stockpile. The Word of God was given to us so that it might be given away.

Let me explain it this way.

While Moses led Israel across the desert, God miraculously fed them manna that fell from heaven each day. It strengthened and sustained them. Do you remember the one and only stipulation? Each day, take only enough for that day. Do not hoard or try to store it up. If you do, it will rot and be full of worms. You mean heavenly manna can actually sour and be infested by worms? Absolutely! What a shame that churches line the landscape of our nation, but on any given weekend they are only partially filled. The same people attend week after week, stuffing themselves on the manna of God. The manna leads us to eternal life and too often we share it with no one. Think about that for a moment. We receive information so powerful that it releases us out of the grip of an eternal hell and we do not share that information with anyone else. How bizarre is that?

One Saturday morning I decided to attend the senior adults' monthly meeting. We all had breakfast together and I made my rounds going from table to table visiting with everyone. I could tell they were delighted I was there. We then all moved to the other end of the room and they entered into a song service of old hymns. After a few songs, they were all seated. Someone had been assigned to share a Bible teaching that morning and as I looked around the room I kept asking myself, "Why? Why are we all gathered together again for another Bible study? It's nice for all of us to be together, but isn't there something more?" They'd been doing this same thing for fifty years, and it bothered me. I was wondering if something was wrong with *me*. Am I not spiritual? I'm the Pastor and I'm irritated by their Bible study. Again, why?

As the Bible study was being taught that morning, I drifted into deep thought.

My question was, "Why do we focus so much of our energy on stuffing ourselves with more and more of the Bible, when so many people have never heard or simply don't understand it?"

The latest statistics say that 95 percent of Christians have never personally led anyone to Christ. That one statistic shows that something has gone horribly wrong with our religious system. We've turned Christ's church into a "me" religion. It's unthinkable for us to admit that we are very much like the Pharisees.

They put to memory a massive amount of scripture. Yet, Jesus said to them, "You don't even know scripture or the power of God." They were stuffed so full of God's Law that it rotted on the inside and it poisoned them. A diabolical poison flowed out of those "church people."

The most destructive people Jesus encountered were the religious. As I stated earlier, the greatest enemy of Christ's church is the religious. They have fallen into the ranks of the "lukewarm." They are the ones that God will spew out of his mouth on the Day of Judgment, and it's the most dangerous place you can find yourself. Satan's most effective weapon against the church is deceiving people who have gorged themselves on the Word of God and have made Christ and His sacrifice a common thing. When something is common, we have lost the sense of its value.

> *Satan's most effective weapon against the church is deceiving people who have gorged themselves on the Word of God and have made Christ and His sacrifice a common thing.*

The writer of Hebrews tells us that anyone who has tasted the salvation of the Lord and yet considers it a common thing, tramples the blood of Christ under foot. That's a serious offense. We are not to take the words of Christ and turn them into self-consumption.

What I truly believe is that the Christian veterans, the older generation, are the most spiritually untapped resource on earth. They are looking for a cause and the church hasn't given them one. There are 60-year-olds who believe their best days are over. Their abilities are no longer needed. In reality, they are in the prime of life to change the world.

White-Haired Warrior

When we read the amazing story of Caleb, from one perspective, he might seem to be bragging...but take a closer look:

> "...just as the LORD promised, he has kept me alive for forty-five years ... so here I am today, eighty-five years old! I am still as strong today as the day Moses sent me out; I'm just as vigorous to go out to battle now as I was then. Now give me this hill country that the LORD promised me that day. You yourself heard then that the Anakites were there and their cities were large and fortified, but the LORD helping me, I will drive them out just as he said." Joshua 14:10-12 (NIV)

Notice that three times he mentions the name of Yahweh.

"The LORD promised... The LORD promised... the LORD helping me."

Here is a man who has learned to trust in the promises of God and stake his whole future on them. He knows what it is like to have the LORD help him, and he is trusting that the LORD will continue to do so. It sounds like bragging, but it is faith, bragging on the power of God to keep his promises. I like that kind of faith!

Why did he want Mount Hebron? Caleb and the other spies had walked hundreds of miles up to the northernmost part of Canaan and back again. His feet had treaded the whole country. Of all of Palestine that could have been his for the asking, why did he pick Hebron? I think he wanted Hebron because it's where the Anakite giants lived that had so terrified his fellow scouts forty years prior. "We looked like grasshoppers in their eyes," they whimpered. But Caleb said, "Bring them on. They look like grasshoppers in the eyes of God. They're no match for the LORD!" Forty-five years before, he had counseled Joshua, saying, "Their protection is gone, but the LORD is with us."

Now forty-five years later he had a chance to prove God's faithfulness. The giants represent the enemies of conquest and Caleb is ready to take on the giants that destroyed the future of God's blessing in millions of lives. He was a white-haired warrior with great experience and wisdom in life. He saw himself as a watchman over the younger generation. He was preparing to fight, not for himself, but for the children and grandchildren of his nation, so that they would have a bright future.

That's what we need from our older generation. We need them to lead the way. It's when we look at our Christ-given mission and say, "I'll march through the gates of hell and take on the demonic powers that want to destroy our children and grandchildren. After decades of being in church, why do I still need a certain style of worship that appeals to me? What about a lost young generation that would be attracted to a totally different style?" What we should be saying is, "Come on, worship team. Rock the house!

Shake the rafters if that's what it takes. I'll gladly wear earplugs, while tears stream down my face, watching the young fill our buildings and being introduced to Jesus Christ. Then I can go home and enjoy listening to the Gaither Vocal Band all week long. Why do I need to continually sit in a senior adult Bible study week after week when I could be spending time loving, mentoring, and pouring into the young? Why do I care how people come dressed for church? Why would I care if a teenager sits in the service with a baseball cap on or covered in tattoos? Why do I care if the whole religious applecart is turned upside down? It's not about *my* likes or *my* dislikes or *my* schedule. This isn't about tradition. This isn't about me!"

Just two weeks before, I watched one of our ushers grab a young man as he was entering our auditorium wearing a baseball cap. The usher rudely yanked the cap from his head, informing him he would not enter the Lord's House wearing a hat. That was the first and last experience that young man had at our church. That is a prime example of losing sight of the big picture. A stupid baseball cap could be the difference between someone spending an eternity in heaven or hell. This is spiritual warfare – the deadliest and most vital of all wars.

I want to be just like Caleb, who prepared the way for the young. We desperately need a shift in church culture in our nation and it must take place now!

Temple Worship vs. the Marketplace

When Jesus started his three-year ministry, the world was also in desperate need of a paradigm shift. At that time, everything spiritual revolved around the Temple. It was a powerful institution. Then, after the day of Pentecost, everything changed. Peter stood on a street corner and preached about the fulfillment of the

Messiah, Jesus Christ. Three thousand people believed and made a commitment to become Christ-followers.

In a very short time, thousands more had become followers. The focus was moving from the Temple to homes, the marketplace and to the countryside.

The priests and devout Jews saw the only religious system they had ever known begin to slip away. What they had enjoyed for so long was their "ethnically pure" movement and the security of a routine, which was now being threatened. They hated the change that was now taking place. It would never be the same again. The Pharisees' sin was they cared more about their tradition and positions than they cared about people being introduced to a God who could save them.

> *Much of the American church has centered itself around temple worship, making it all about the church instead of being all about the world.*

It's easy to fall prey to such deception. Much of the American church has centered itself around temple worship, making it all about the church instead of being all about the world.

Before I knew it, the Bible study was over and the leader was asking everyone to stand for the closing prayer. Everyone standing so abruptly awoke me from my deep thoughts. As I stood among that group of people, they all had their heads bowed. I looked around and realized I was standing with a group of people who had the potential to change the world, but I also knew they would have to change their religious philosophies. Many of them would have to change a belief system that had been instilled in them for many years.

I walked out of that meeting greatly saddened because I knew most of them would not be willing to join me in the journey on which I was about to lead them. I wanted them and needed them desperately.

The vision and direction had already been launched and there was no turning back. At that moment, I felt the enormous weight of responsibility on my shoulders to lead this change.

I heard a quote many years ago by James Bryant Conant that said, "Behold the turtle: He only makes progress when he sticks his neck out." My neck was stretched out about as far as it could be stretched. I was sure hoping it was for progress and not for the chopping block.

That Saturday morning I drove to one of my favorite coffee shops to finish up my message for the weekend. The senior adult breakfast had really messed me up. I couldn't even focus on my message. I was so consumed with why there are so few willing to give up *their* church traditions and routines to advance the Kingdom. The enemy continues invading our nation while the church has one more pot luck dinner.

The Bean Patch

Sitting in the corner of the coffee shop, I was scanning through many different Old Testament stories, when I unintentionally came across one I had completely forgotten: The story of the bean patch, found in 2 Samuel 23:11-17.

It was at a time when Israel was struggling for survival. They would plant their crops but at harvest time their archenemy, the Philistines, would sweep down like a swarm of locusts, leaving the Israelites with nothing. It was threatening their survival. It was now harvest time again and they were placing small Israelite troops to stand guard, defending their fields from the enemy. In one particular bean patch, they stationed a small band of soldiers. Just as they had anticipated, a large number of Philistines came running toward the field. When this small band of Israelite soldiers saw how large in number their enemy was, they ran for their lives. That is, all but one man whose name was Shammah. Instead of running, he stood in the middle of the field, dug his feet firmly into the ground and drew his sword. As the Philistines came upon him, he swung that sword with all of his might.

The Lord came upon him and he slew them all.

As I read that story I wondered, "Why would anyone risk their life for a bean patch? Why fight for something so insignificant?"

I kept staring at this passage on the screen of my laptop. I wondered, if I had been there that day, what would I have done? Would I have run with all the others or would I have stood shoulder to shoulder with Shammah? I think I would have run because I'm definitely not willing to die for a few beans. If most were not willing to die for a bean patch, why was Shammah? At that very moment I saw it. He had the ability to see the big picture. His fellow soldiers only saw the bean patch they were standing in, but Shammah was looking far beyond. He was being driven by a vision of the future. He knew his enemy wouldn't stop at that bean patch. They would just keep coming. If they took this patch, they would take the next, and the next, and the next. They would eventually take his home, then his wife and kids and then the whole city.

Shammah wasn't fighting for a bean patch. He was fighting for the freedom of future generations.

As I leaned back in my chair, with an extreme heaviness, my questions were, "Are there any Calebs or Shammahs left in the world today? Where have all the great leaders of the church gone?"

Can I Call You Caleb?

A few months later God answered that prayer. I had recently performed a funeral service for an elderly woman that I didn't know very well. Her husband was in his early eighties and had never been a follower of Christ. He was a crusty, hard-working, old farmer-type. He had always been a little harsh and not one to show much affection to his wife or children. He also had never made time for God or the church. The loss of his wife had shaken him and left him feeling empty. Her death made him think, for the first time, about eternity. He started attending church on Sunday mornings. He came alone and sat in the back by himself. It wasn't long until, one Sunday morning, he made his way to the front and accepted Christ into his life.

That day I witnessed one of the most dramatic transformations I have ever seen. He became one of the kindest and most loving people I have ever met. He volunteered as a greeter and it became his greatest passion. He took greeting people to another level. This wasn't a job, but full-out ministry. It was the highlight of his week. When you walked in the doors of our church he made you feel like the most loved person on the planet. Every Sunday morning, when that eighty-three-year-old finished greeting at the door, he would walk to the front of the auditorium and sit in the youth section – one of the greatest sights I've ever seen. These teenagers gathered around him before and after church. He quickly became the most popular man in the congregation. He was also the biggest supporter of our new vision to reach the young. He was so emotionally moved by wanting everyone to experience the Christ that had changed his life that I honestly can't remember a service where he did not cry.

It was at this same time that we were being very intentional in making changes that would attract and directly communicate to a young generation. The rumbling started among the older crowd. I could feel the uneasiness growing within this group. It only takes a handful of negative people to kill a vision. But what I witnessed is that it only takes one person to champion a cause. He became the "Caleb" of our church. As a younger man he had not raised his family in the church, nor had he ever desired to follow Christ, but now everything had changed. He became the white-haired warrior who helped move this vision forward, simply by being so excited about the possibility of a young generation filling our church.

He was a new convert with no preconceived ideas of what we should do or shouldn't do in church. He didn't care if we sang hymns or if we rocked out with the latest music in worship. He didn't care about the decor of the building. He couldn't have cared less about traditions that we had practiced for the past seventy-five years. All he cared about was the vision the pastor had cast to reach a young generation, and his attitude simply said, "Let's just get it done." It was like the Lord was letting me know that yes, there are many Calebs who are willing to fight for the greatest cause on earth – winning, training, and releasing the next generation.

Don't ever let age count you out. People turning fifty today have half their adult lives ahead of them.

The fifty-plus crowd in this nation could lead a revolution to reinvent church culture and actually win the masses. Don't let anyone tell you you're out of step or too old-fashioned to make a difference. That's simply a decision you make. Don't let yourself get old. Stay in the game. It's a lot more exciting. The fastest growing population of people joining Facebook is grandmothers – used primarily for stalking their kids and grandkids. Through Facebook, grandmothers are almost omniscient. It's like the all-seeing eye. They know every move you and your family make.

People fifty-five years and older are more active in online financing, shopping, and entertainment than those under fifty-five. Americans over fifty control a gargantuan share of the personal wealth in the United States. This group's influence is enormous. The average American over the age of fifty will buy seven more cars in his lifetime.

Talk about power and influence – this group, moving in the right direction, could rock the nations. Come on, it's time for some "Calebs" to rise up and lead!

Chapter 6

A Strange New Culture

Kay and I decided that we would break the mold of the temple in our lives in the same way the apostle Paul broke out of the confines of the temple in his life. We were both surprised by how deep religious traditions controlled the way we thought. We turned our eyes toward the fields and started befriending the very ones we had targeted to reach. More than anything, we wanted to enter into their world instead of asking them to enter ours.

We opened up our home to high school and college students every night of the week. We cooked for them, made cookies and popcorn, and watched movies. On weekends we made a deliberate decision not to hang out with people our own age but to go and do what the students were doing. I wanted to learn everything I possibly could about them.

What Happened to the Generation Gap?

Just like Paul, we entered their world. Just as every missionary on the foreign field fears being rejected by the people they are trying to reach, it was also a great fear of ours. We continued inviting them to our home and found ourselves going out with them on weekends to movies, dinners, concerts, parties and sporting events. We were sure we would wear out our welcome very quickly. I was prepared to be ignored by them and I certainly wouldn't blame them because of the generation gap between us.

That was the buzzword when I was a kid growing up. For two decades that was a phrase on everybody's lips, "Generation Gap." There was a real animosity between the young generation and the older generation. The early seventies was a time of great national turbulence. The young generation of our country rebelled and they walked away from traditionalism. They were anti-war, anti-government and anti-establishment. The hippie movement was nothing more than a radical way of saying, to an older generation, that they could take their world and shove it! The young and the old did not see eye-to-eye. The young literally saw themselves at war with the culture their parents and grandparents had created. There was a very real generational gap, and it was one of the most disturbing times in our country. The young began to lose respect for their authority figures and it was during this time that the phrase "my old man" became popular – an incredibly disrespectful term referring to their fathers. Never in the history of America had the youth of our nation ever rebelled at this widespread level.

I remember that time very well. What I found so interesting, as I interacted with these students in coffee shops or restaurants, talking about world affairs or the purpose of life or spiritual issues, was that they were far different from my generation. When I was twenty I vividly remember not wanting to hear the advice from the elderly, that is, anyone who was over forty. We wanted to make our own way in life and certainly didn't need the input from some old person. What I quickly learned is that this generation was far different from what I expected. They loved having deep intellectual conversations and they hung on my every word. They wanted my input and my advice. They wanted Kay and me to talk about our marriage, ministry, and our family. They wanted to hear about our family vacations, our parents and how we were raising our three boys.

It caught me off guard at first. These young men wanted to learn from me. They craved my attention and time. Why? I had never really thought about this before, but I hadn't heard the term "generation gap" in a long time because in this culture it no longer exists. Today there is no such thing.

As I sat at the table, surrounded by a group of twenty-year-olds, I was totally immersed into their world. I listened to their conversation and I suddenly understood why this generation is so different from mine. Their parents and grandparents were the products of the sixties and seventies. These Baby Boomer parents came out of the age of Aquarius, the era of drugs, sex, rock and roll, and on top of that the Vietnam War that had left severe scars on that generation. So many of them grew up and became parents who were still battling alcoholism and drug addiction in record numbers. It was this generation that now had the highest divorce rate in history. The family became fractured to the point where today one out of every two children in the United States will live in a single-parent family at some time before they reach age eighteen.

Through the fracturing of family life, a new phrase surfaced – "dysfunctional families." In all of the family turmoil, these Baby Boomers acquired wealth higher than any other generation. They were moving into bigger houses with two-car garages, buying all kinds of recreational equipment – boats, camping trailers, new cars. They went on expensive vacations and were going out to eat in record numbers. These Baby Boomer parents were also raised with a high respect for God and the church. They were very religious and they took their families to church every week. It was a time of abundance, and churches across the country were erecting big beautiful buildings in which to worship. With unprecedented prosperity they became the "ME" generation. It was a self-consumed culture, and that mentality also infiltrated the church world.

Through the seventies and eighties the church lost its focus and turned inward. Its highest priority was to meet the needs of church people instead of meeting the needs of the world. Everyone dressed up in their coats and ties and the ladies wore their beautiful Sunday dresses. Church congregations looked like they were filled with perfect Christian families. The outside world truly believed church was for the highly religious, and they certainly wouldn't fit in or be welcomed. This became the image that was conveyed to the outside world. Church attendance became more about social status and keeping up a good appearance than anything else.

It was their children who watched the inconsistencies. They would go to church, worship God, and go home, where complete mayhem broke out. These children saw a religious institution that claimed God changes lives, yet saw no life-changing power. They viewed the church as outdated, old-fashioned, self-consumed, boring, and powerless. The Baby Boomers' kids were disillusioned by a God who their parents worshiped on Sunday, while their home-life was falling apart.

As I sat at the table listening to these college students, I found that they were very informed about world conditions, politics, and their own views of religion. I loved being around them. They were so full of life, energy, and excitement. As I walked out of the restaurant that day I thought, "These are the people who will change the world and I want to help them do it."

An Unlikely Church Staff

I began diligently working on putting together a staff of people who could help me reach our vision. The obstacle of staffing a church is always money, and we didn't have much.

This may be where we need to change our thinking. Why focus on paid staff when we have an army of volunteers in front us? It's their calling and passion and it brings tremendous joy into their lives. It's their spiritual purpose. It's their cause. One of the things I complained about for so many years was that we just couldn't get people to volunteer and faithfully commit. It was like everybody was just flaky – not dependable. Everything was half done. What I later came to understand was that *this* was the church culture we had created. The reason why: I always felt guilty putting demands on people who already had full time jobs. So, you get what you expect. Expect little you will get little in return.

Think about this: If our church is dry, boring, not growing, seeing few salvations and few baptisms, and has drab worship, then why would anyone give their best in that kind of environment?

> *If our church is dry, boring, not growing, seeing few salvations and few baptisms, and has drab worship, then why would anyone give their best in that kind of environment?*

While sorting through all of this, our oldest son, Dustin, was about to graduate from Southwestern Assemblies of God University. Our youth pastor at the time, who had been on our staff for ten years, had just resigned to pastor a church in Birmingham, Alabama. Dustin and I had a very serious conversation about the possibility of his coming onboard and filling that position. I explained to him the risk that was involved in a pastor hiring his own son. The responsibility of the next student ministries' pastor was going to be huge because this demographic was going to be the bull's eye of our focus as a church. What we were about to create was a system where young people could meet God and be radically changed for the rest of their lives. We weren't just interested in a good youth ministry, but something spiritually that would systemically move them from one stage of life to the next. It would take them from children's ministry to middle school to high school to college and then into a career and family life.

Having twelve years of experience as a youth pastor, I have always been very concerned with the church's drop-out rate of graduating high school seniors. Once they graduated they seemed misplaced in the church. They become detached and eventually disappear. The one church statistic that should scare the church to death is that 68 percent of kids who are raised in church will leave the church after high school and will not raise their kids in church. We are not talking about our unchurched neighborhood kids. We're talking about our own kids that we've raised in church and by church people. That should be an eye-opener that the church is not speaking their language. If that's the case, then the death of the American church is not far in the future.

As Dustin and I continued talking about the job description for a new student pastor, I sat there looking at a 22-year-old, who in my eyes was just a kid with absolutely no experience. I couldn't help but wonder if I was setting him up for failure. We had a vacation scheduled for the beginning of the summer to Gulf Shores, Alabama, our favorite vacation spot. It was a great time for us to really think through all of the logistics.

One day we were driving along the coast and talking through some of the difficulties of building a great student ministry. One of the obstacles for us was that we had no one to lead worship. I asked him if he knew of a friend from college who would want to help lead worship for student ministries for the summer. Immediately he said, "Jonathan. He leads worship for the chapel services from time to time and he's really good." I had Dustin call him and offer him an internship for the summer. Jonathan loved the idea and said he would be in Albuquerque the day we arrived back from vacation. When we returned, he was there waiting for us. I was greeted by a very loud and outgoing 20-year-old. I could tell this kid had never met a stranger. The next day we sat down together and I told them that their mission for the summer was to launch a college ministry. They were to build a leadership team and by the end of the summer the goal was to hit an attendance of one hundred students. In passing, I just threw out an incentive, "If you reach the goal, I'll take you to the best steak house in town and buy you anything you want."

They jumped at the challenge with determination – as if it was a done deal – high-fiving each other like I had just lost the bet. They had no idea that college ministry was the hardest ministry to build. Few churches ever do it successfully. We had tried many times before with marginal results. I had just given them "Mission Impossible." I was just thankful they were young and dumb enough to think it could be done. Throughout the summer we started building a base of young volunteers, interns, and part-time staff. I was looking everywhere for talented young men and women, just waiting for someone to give them an opportunity... and of course for little money.

My middle son, whose name is also Jonathan, was playing high school football at the time. They were playing in the state championship game and that morning they were having an all-school pep rally. Kay and I slipped into the gymnasium packed with students. As we were seated, the student body president was at center court with a microphone and he had that place rocking. I'd never seen anyone with that kind of energy. He was electrifying. I can remember thinking, "This kid would be an amazing student pastor." Two weeks later I walked into my house and Adam, the student body president, was sitting in our den watching TV with my boys. I struck up a conversation with him and found out that his parents had been in ministry for many years. In a short amount of time, Adam joined our staff for part-time pay.

A few weeks later our boys had invited a bunch of their friends over to watch a movie. They all gathered in our basement. Kay and I cooked up a huge batch of chocolate chip cookies. I grabbed a gallon of milk and headed to the basement.

The lights were down low and I stopped to let my eyes adjust to the darkness. I could tell that the movie was very suspenseful and everyone was glued to the TV. I was standing in the back of the room waiting for the right time to put the tray of cookies on the coffee table. Just at that moment, one of the boys saw a shadow of someone standing directly behind them. It startled him so badly that he jumped out of his seat and yelled. I stumbled backwards and almost dropped the whole tray.

He went on and on about how that old man scared him to death! My first thought was, "Who's he calling an old man?" Well, that was the night I met Derek for the first time. This kid had an attitude with a chip on his shoulder. His parents had just gone through a divorce and he was angry. He had major trust issues and he wasn't interested in letting people get too close. Just listening to him talk made me laugh…I couldn't help it. I'd never heard anyone so sarcastic. He absolutely had no filter on his mouth, and he made it very well known to everyone that he was an atheist. The thought of God was ridiculous to him, but for whatever reason, I was intrigued with this kid. Standing in front of me was a very hurt, confused, and angry young man. He was the epitome of what this young, lost generation looked like. Little did I know that I was going to spend the next few years with this group of guys. I prayed for God to help me put a ministry team together to reach this generation and this is what I get: Dustin, who has no preaching experience – Jonathan, who was from a "Holiness" background and whose specialty is singing old hymns – Adam, who was an overly hyperactive high school student body president – and Derek, a self-proclaimed atheist. WOW! What an unlikely bunch. My thought was, "It couldn't get much worse than this." They were nothing but inexperienced kids. No credentials, no experience, no resumes.

I was thinking I needed a highly experienced associate pastor. What I really wanted was an executive pastor like every successful pastor has. Instead, I ended up with a rag tag group of guys. What can a bunch of nineteen and twenty-year-olds do?

After working side by side with them for several months, I answered my own question. They will turn the world upside down. They always have and they always will.

To save money, three of them lived at our house with our family. Literally, we were together 24/7. We built a camaraderie with one another that is rare. We respected and loved each other, but most of all, we had fun!

The average age of my pastoral staff was twenty-three. And I knew our congregation thought I had absolutely lost my mind. Going through this process, many times I questioned my own sanity. They were loud, immature, obnoxious, and would embarrass you to death in public. On one occasion we all went to see "The Da Vinci Code." It was opening night and the theater was packed. There had been a lot of controversy over how the movie portrayed Christianity. Just minutes before it started, Jonathan got up out of his seat without saying a word and walked to the front of the jam-packed theater. He raised his hands and whistled to get everyone's attention. Then, he proceeded to tell the audience, "Ladies and gentlemen, the show you are about to see is fictional. It is not a true story, so do not leave here believing this as truth. Thank you for your attention and enjoy the show." He stirred up a hornets' nest. Half of the place was clapping and cheering and the other half were booing and yelling things back at him. I thought he was going to start a riot. Then he came back and plopped down next to me as I was sliding under my seat in embarrassment.

No matter where we went, it was always the same. A few nights later we were invited to a party at a church member's home.

All the long-term members had been invited. It was a formal gathering where everyone was dressed up and dignified. That is, until we walked in the door. Immediately, Jonathan saw Adam, ran in and jumped all the way up on his shoulders while letting out an extremely loud yell. This was all taking place in the foyer of their home. I looked around the room and every church member was frozen in their tracks. The place went silent. It was an extremely awkward moment. Every eye turned to me as if to ask, "Are you kidding? Is this really our pastoral staff?"

Well, needless to say we had a lot of sit-down meetings on how to act and what was proper to say and not to say. Leading this highly spirited clan was like herding cats. Every time they were handed a microphone on stage I cringed and tore holes into the seat cushions, not knowing what was about to come out of their mouths.

On the positive side, this young group was like workhorses. They didn't tire. They were young and single with time on their hands. Their energy levels were remarkably high. Creative ideas were flying and they were working late into the night to make their ideas happen. Their passion, energy, and excitement was contagious. They lit a fire under me. Their young minds and technological abilities took us places my mind had never gone.

Within two months, I began to see their remarkable talents starting to shine. Constantly we were talking about teaching styles, music, and creative elements that would be appealing to the unchurched. By the end of the summer the youth ministry was flourishing and our college group was growing at a rate I didn't think possible. They hit over one hundred students before the summer was over, and yes, I was out a lot of money at the most expensive steakhouse in town.

Energized By Young Leadership

The atmosphere of our church began to change drastically. Kay and I attended every student service and found ourselves working side by side with them every night of the week. It was like a student take-over. And yes, the complaining was rising with the older crowd. Comments started emerging, "The pastor's turning our church into a youth church. He's forgotten all about us." In reality, we were just staying true to the vision. The vision was manifesting itself in physical form, and we were reaching young people.

Working with this remarkable young group I began to realize why the Bible says, "Don't let anyone look down on you because you are young."

Most scholars believe David was somewhere between thirteen and seventeen years old when he killed Goliath. He was a kid who did what no other Israelite warrior could do. He took on, undoubtedly, the greatest warrior in the world. The three Hebrew children were just that – children. They were young boys who changed the course of a nation because of their bravery and their willingness to die for a cause.

Today, the Muslims have made a conscious decision to focus on training their young, and they are the fastest growing religion in the world.

The Mormons have done the very same thing. They expect 18-year-olds, 19-year-olds, and 20-year-olds to commit two years of their lives to be missionaries somewhere in the world. And because of this they are rapidly growing all around the globe. Adversely, in the Protestant church, we seem to ignore our youth and certainly don't make them the focus of our interest. It's the reason we are declining in numbers.

Our own nation has put so much faith in the young that we put them on the front lines to defend our country. Yet most churches today see the young as immature people who haven't earned the right to lead. The problem is that we haven't taken the time to mentor them and turn them loose. The young are the greatest resource the church has today.

> *The young are the greatest resource the church has today.*

I found that out firsthand. After six months of working alongside of them, I realized I was working with, hands-down, the greatest leaders with whom I had ever been associated.

The foundation of our leadership team and a culture-shift were quickly being formed. We began to experience a unified vision that generated momentum and enthusiasm. It's the power of "teamwork."

It was through this process of working with this young group, and with the rest of our staff, that I really understood the importance of unity. If you don't have it, it will short-circuit your ability to advance. When building your team, consider these factors.

Four Vital Characteristics For Great Team Members

1. Team Spirit – You don't want people on your team who create turf wars. It's tunnel-vision ministry. They are hypersensitive and become hard to work with. They make issues over things like, it's my night, my room, they are my people, my time slot – as if they are in competition with other ministries

and leaders. Often they are functioning from an offended spirit as if they are the victim. They overlook the big picture and become "My Ministry" driven instead of "Us Ministry" centered. This kind of person drains the entire team. Valuable team members are willing to be flexible and compliant and to cross ministry lines when asked to help another ministry succeed. Instead of being overly protective and sensitive, they are willing to put their ministry on hold for the overall good of the church – not just for their individual ministry.

2. A Strong Work Ethic – We simply rely on people having the sense of responsibility and inner drive needed to complete the work. These leaders are passionate about Christ and people, and willing to do whatever it takes to accomplish the vision. They do not have a 9 to 5 workday mentality, but have the passion and excitement to get a job done...even if it takes working until 2 a.m. because they are committed to the cause.

3. A Healthy Personal Life – Ministry leaders deal with a lot of messiness in other people's lives. It would make it very difficult to maintain the level of ministry required if they were not personally living healthy lives spiritually, emotionally, and physically.

4. Loyalty – It is imperative, in any organization, that team members be dedicated to the vision, organization, senior leadership, and the team. As a pastor, I am committed to stand by staff members who have fallen spiritually and morally, doing my best to restore them. But when it comes to disloyalty, which is biblically classified as rebellion, they are fired with no opportunity to return. Disloyalty is the deadliest of all sins and one that all of us will deal with as church leaders. No one likes to believe it can happen to them, but it will. No one is exempt. Even God experienced disloyalty when Lucifer

rebelled. Jesus experienced disloyalty from Judas. I'm sure King David was completely taken by surprise when Absalom, his son, took up arms and marched against him to overthrow his throne.

> *By all means, keep loyal people close and immediately detach from anyone with a trace of disloyalty.*

I can't think of any other sin that is so destructive and divisive in the body of Christ. By all means, keep loyal people close and immediately detach from anyone with a trace of disloyalty.

Teamwork, Enormous Power

Teamwork is a familiar word that's thrown around a lot. However, most of us are unaware of its true impact. Think about the concept of "teamwork" for a moment. It's difficult to be successful in any area of life without it – whether in marriage, ministry, business, or even in our own personal lives. In the end, teamwork can be summed up in five short words: "We believe in each other."

Teamwork is one of the greatest powers God designed within humanity. We see this throughout the Bible. In the beginning, God created Adam and said, "It is not good that man should be alone." He created a partner, companion, friend, and mate. In other words, He created a teammate.

When a man and woman team up in marriage, it is one of the greatest forces on earth. The reason why marriage has such a high failure rate is because couples still see themselves as individuals, demanding their own way and their own rights. They live out their marriage as two separate people under the same roof, fighting for their own needs to be met. That's the opposite of how God designed it to function. God's Word tells us that when two enter into marriage they become one. They team up, working together as one, with one vision, one direction, and one purpose. Two people set aside their own desires and plans to merge with each other. Over time, individual dreams begin to fade and a team vision is formed. The beauty of this merger is that we add to our lives all the strengths of our spouse and vice versa. It's a team concept, "We are better together." When marriage follows God's design, the marriage team becomes a force to be reckoned with.

Noah teamed up with his family for over a hundred years and built the ark which saved humanity.

Nehemiah teamed up with a small band of men to rebuild the walls of Jerusalem. Everyone they encountered was convinced it was impossible and they were foolish for attempting such a feat. Yet, they accomplished it in a remarkable 52 days.

Gideon teamed up with 300 farmers and herdsmen who had never been trained in warfare, yet defeated a massive army of thousands.

Jesus teamed up with twelve disciples. Paul teamed up with Silas. Barnabas teamed up with Mark. It's amazing how any time people team up for a cause, the world changes.

It's been said that teamwork is the fuel that allows common people to produce uncommon results.

In the Old Testament there's the fascinating story of the Tower of Babel. It's a picture of what can be achieved by a team of people who are united.

> "But the Lord came down to see the city and the
> tower the people were building. The Lord said, "If
> as one people speaking the same language they have

begun to do this, then nothing they plan to do will be impossible for them." Genesis 11:5-6 (NIVUK)

When people team up aggressively and passionately for one common purpose, God said that nothing would be impossible to them.

What a statement. Why? Because they were working in unity with each other, even though it was for an evil cause. One of the most fascinating, God-designed principles is the power of agreement and unity called teamwork. It's the FUEL that allows common people to produce uncommon results!

The animal world illustrates this amazing principle.

Horse Power

Back in the late 1800's, horse-pulling contests were a favorite at the county fair. At one particular fair, the first-place horse moved a sled weighing 4500 pounds. The runner-up pulled 4000 pounds. Later that evening the proud owners of these two horses were having dinner. They wondered how much their horses could pull if they were teamed up. So they hitched them together and loaded the sled. To everyone's surprise, the horses were able to pull over 12,000 pounds. That's 3,500 pounds more than they had pulled on their own. Two horses teaming up will do what three horses could do individually. That's SYNERGY! It's the combining of forces.

Synergy creates a mathematical formula that cannot be explained. 1 + 1 = 3! It's the same power the Bible teaches that operates through believers. One can do great things, two can do extraordinary things, but three or more can do miraculous things. Look at what Jesus said,

"Again, truly I tell you that if two of you on earth
agree about anything they ask for, it will be done for
them by my Father in heaven. For where two or three
gather in my name, there am I with them." Matthew
18:19-20 (NIV)

This biblical principle can be referred to as synergy, agreement or
teamwork, but it doesn't really matter what we call it as long as
we get unified in vision and purpose. A unified team determines
success at any level.

Human Limitations

I recently visited London during the Summer Olympics. The
entire globe was focused on this one city while athletes came
from every country with hopes and dreams of being the best in
the world.

Each morning I would go online and check the medal standings
for an updated list of each country and how many gold, silver,
or bronze medals had been won. In some ways, the whole
world stopped as we watched them compete and listened to
their emotional stories of overcoming obstacles and surpassing
insurmountable odds to be the best in the world. Day after day
new world records were set with a new standard for everyone
to pursue.

Have you ever thought about this? When do we come to the
end of our human physical capacity? Doesn't there come a time
when the body reaches its limit? Don't you think the day will
come when setting new world records will be a rarity because
you can only push the human body so far? It doesn't work that
way. Olympic Games have been going on for over two thousand
years, and for two thousand years athletes have continued to

105

find new ways to run faster, jump higher, and go further than anyone before.

Over the course of these past Summer Olympics, over forty new world records were set. When does mankind hit the wall of advancement? Never!

As long as athletes team up with other athletes and coaches, and then add in passion, synergy kicks in and nothing they plan to do will be impossible for them. They will continue to reach new heights.

> *Teamwork is more than just teaming up with people, but teaming up with the right people.*

Teamwork is more than just teaming up with people, but teaming up with the *right* people.

Chapter 7

Dreams or Excuses

I would attend church conferences and hear about all kinds of great new ideas that were working for big churches. I would then bring those new, exciting ideas back to our church and launch it as our new vision. We would rally everyone together and kick off a campaign with great enthusiasm. We did this numerous times and each time, after about six months, it had already completely fizzled out. I didn't understand true God-given vision. When I sat in the C3 conference service on that first night I experienced something I had never been exposed to before. It wasn't an idea. It was a burning of the heart. I wept. Something ached on the inside and it resonated with me. When I experienced it, felt it, and saw it, immediately I knew the vision – to redesign our church structure to reach a young generation. I knew it was the purpose of my existence. For the first time, I understood vision.

> *Vision is birthed but it has no death.*

Vision is birthed but it has no death. It's what you're willing to live and die for. Vision is the anchor that holds you steady when no one else believes what's in your heart or in your words. Vision is unshakable even when church members are frustrated and threaten to leave the church with their money. Vision doesn't die because of criticism or obstacles. Vision lives when man connects with God's invisible force to advance His Kingdom. If you have a calling and a vision from God, you had better believe there will be opposition from the enemy camp.

When I boldly stated my God-given vision and dream,

> "We are going to be a church
> of all ages
> reaching a young generation"

I had no idea that statement could be so divisive and unpopular.

Effective leaders don't lead by popular demand. Many times leaders must swim against the tide, crossing the line of conformity. God may be calling you to lead your troops off the known map into uncharted territory. Nothing can be more fearful and exciting all at the same time.

For the first time in fourteen years of pastoring, I had a vision for which I was willing to risk everything. I implemented this vision statement in every conversation, every sermon and at every luncheon.

You can never grow tired in talking about it. You talk about it when you get up…and you're still talking about it when you go to bed. Each new day is an opportunity to advance the dream.

As I read through the Bible I found that visions and dreams are interchangeable terms, which reminded me of a quote I love:

"All men dream: but not equally. Those who dream by night in the dusty recesses of their minds wake in the day to find that it was vanity: but the dreamers of the day are dangerous men, for they may act their dream with open eyes to make it possible."

— T.E. Lawrence

What's Your Dream?

What is that one dream that you would be embarrassed to tell your spouse or best friend because it just seems too far beyond your ability? It sounds silly that you think you could do something out of the ordinary, much less achieve what few have ever accomplished.

Where do you think dreams come from? Dreams of greatness. Dreams of building a church that will literally change a city. Dreams of ending world hunger. Dreams of taking the Gospel to the darkest places on earth. The dream of turning a small, declining church into a place where the poor, addicted, abandoned, and the hurting find new life through Christ. Those are dreams birthed within us by the Creator. God's desire is to flow through you so that you might reach your created purpose. Your dream needs to be fulfilled so that the world might be won for Christ. God is your biggest fan and wants you to reach for the impossible! Our dreams fail for only one reason: We focus on our own human weaknesses. But it has never been about us. It has always been about what God wants to do through us. We are nothing more than a vessel that God will fill and use for His divine purpose.

Think about all the examples in the Bible of how God loves transforming weak and messed-up people to change the world. Adam and Eve were disobedient blame-shifters. Abraham was a liar. Jacob was a schemer. Joseph had somewhat of an "I'm better than you" attitude. Moses made excuses. Saul was jealous. David was an adulterer. Solomon was the wisest fool in the history of the world. Elijah seemed to be somewhat bipolar. Peter definitely had "foot-in-mouth" disease. The list goes on and on.

So many times we become so obsessed with that one glaring weakness that it blinds us from what we are really capable of accomplishing. We are convinced that our dreams are nothing but an unrealistic fantasy. The apostle Paul gives incredible insight on human weakness and divine power.

The Lord spoke to Paul in 2 Corinthians chapter 12, "My grace is sufficient for you, for power is perfected in weakness. Most gladly, therefore, I will rather boast about my weaknesses, so that the power of Christ may dwell in me. Therefore I am well content with weaknesses, with insults, with distresses, with persecutions, with difficulties, for Christ's sake; for when I am weak, then I am strong."

God will always compensate for our weakness. What I've come to believe is that the greater the weakness, the greater His power will be expressed. Your limitations are no match for His divine power. Don't let anything stop your dream.

> *Your limitations are no match for His divine power. Don't let anything stop your dream.*

To dream is the mental picture of what we could achieve. Dreaming is the divine gift of imagination. It is said that all things are created twice – once in our minds and secondly in physical form.

All successful people convert their dreams into goals and goals into reality. If you don't believe in your dream, no one else will.

The Greatest Golf Story Ever Told

One of my favorite stories of dreams coming true is about the pro golfer, Fred Couples, and his good friend Jim Nantz.

One morning, Fred sat on the terrace of his sprawling home and grand estate in Charlotte, North Carolina sipping a cup of coffee. In front of him was his beautiful garden. To his left was the pool – an absolute masterpiece of landscape design. To the right he viewed his tennis courts and perfectly manicured putting and chipping green he had installed a couple of years prior. He spent hundreds of thousands a year to simply keep the practice area in top shape, even though he traveled over 30 weeks per year.

The garage is a museum of luxury automobiles worth over 1 million dollars. That amount of money isn't much for a guy who has earned tens of millions of dollars in his career. As Fred sat, he realized that he was living the dream. "Why is this all happening?" he thought. "Why is it that I've been so fortunate?"

He then started thinking back to his college days in the late 70's at the University of Houston. Fred thought about the good times he and Jim Nantz had as roommates back in Houston. Those were the days! Suddenly something clicked as he thought about Jim. Jim, as strange as it seemed, was at the top of his profession, earning tens of millions in his career also.

As he reflected back on their college days, as silly as it sounds, Fred and Jim would sit around for countless hours in their dorm room role-playing their future.

Back in college Fred was on the golf team at the University of Houston and his roommate was a broadcast journalism student. Many times they had actually acted out Fred winning the Masters at Augusta and Jim holding a hair brush as a microphone, interviewing Fred as he was handed the Master's Green Jacket behind the iconic 18th green. They envisioned a huge crowd of people cheering behind them.

The other guys on their floor told them they were nuts and they should come back to reality. The other guys' opinions didn't matter to them because Jim and Fred loved dreaming the impossible dream.

Before I go on, I just want to point out how absolutely improbable the next part of this story was. The odds of any of this happening, and happening in a way that the whole world would see it play out, is simply a billion to one. But, odds had nothing to do with it.

112

On April 12, 1992, this very dream actually became reality. Just as they had previously enacted the scene, Fred Couples won the Masters. As he walked up the hill, the sports announcer who was to interview him was none other than his old college roommate, Jim Nantz. The exact scene that had been played out so many times when they were just college students actually happened.

When you understand the spiritual principles and the universal laws behind goal-setting you won't feel as though this is really improbable. It is unlikely for most, because most people are not willing to be AVID about the dreams and aspirations God gives them. Most people are not willing to believe in big dreams and to persevere – holding those dreams in their mind until they actually come true.

To be AVID is to be "enthusiastic and vigorous in pursuit of a goal." That is exactly what goal-achievers are. They are AVID and they are on a mission.

To be AVID:

A - Ask yourself what it is you really want.

V - Visualize yourself in possession of your goal.

I - Identify a plan for achieving the goal.

D - Desire the goal constantly, never wavering.

Goal-achievers have meaning in their life; they have purpose and lofty aspirations and vision. The fact that Fred Couples and Jim Nantz actually played out their dream and their dream became reality is not luck and it has nothing to do with chance. They masterminded their future and it manifested results. Dreams are a dime-a-dozen. Anyone can dream, but only those who are AVID will see it come to pass.

It All Starts With A Dream

Remember the famous words, "I have a dream," from Dr. Martin Luther King, Jr. at the Lincoln memorial in Washington, D.C. on August 28, 1963? This immortal speech stirred millions of people. It resonates with every one of us because we all have a dream.

All achievements start with a dream. Your dream is the initial spark which grows into an inferno that eventually makes dreams into reality. All of us need to dream; we need to build the castles we've envisioned in our minds. There is an old saying that we hear people use when they think others are being too lofty in their thoughts: "Don't build castles in sky." But that is not right. Castles are meant to be in the sky. That is where they belong! What we need is to build a foundation to make it real.

Dreams and goals make our life meaningful. Without them life is like a rudderless ship – taking you places you never wanted to go. Dreams and goals are your vision of the future. They are visions of possibilities that help you recognize and seize opportunities.

 "To accomplish great things we must not only act, but also dream; not only plan but also believe." – Anatole

What's Your Excuse?

Isn't it interesting that so many times it's the most unlikely person who ends up succeeding? It is the unattractive one, the one with the odd personality, the one who has no athletic abilities, or the one who was constantly grounded by their parents for poor grades in school. Yet, they are the ones who so often rise to the top.

We all have our own obstacle to overcome. Everyone seems to have that one thing that holds them back from living their dream. It can become an excuse or it can be the very thing that makes victory so sweet. Let me briefly share mine with you.

I grew up in the wide-open plains of west Texas. We lived on the outskirts of Amarillo in a very rural environment. I raised animals and rode horses, gallivanting all over the countryside. I had a great childhood and the best parents on the planet. It was when I started school that I was confronted by my personal nemesis. I loved school and being around all the other kids, but quickly I became aware that something was wrong. I couldn't keep up academically. It wasn't long before everyone knew that I made the worst grades in class.

Week after week those horrible red x's from the teacher's pen bled all over my test papers. I wanted to do well so badly. I wanted the teacher to smile at me like she did with all the other kids. I wanted and needed her approval, but instead I felt like a disappointment.

I had a problem that no one could understand and neither could I. I had a learning disability that professionals at that time did not understand and had yet to even identify. I was suffering from an information-processing disorder. The moment the teacher started talking, it was like her voice became garbled. My mind would drift off to some faraway place. My problem kept me from learning in a lecture-style setting. No matter how hard I tried, my attention span was extremely short. It frustrated me, but I couldn't control it.

By the time I reached the fourth grade I had fallen horribly behind all the other students. I was constantly being pulled out of class for evaluations. They would sit across the table from me and ask the most ridiculous questions. I would think, "Do you think I'm stupid?" I was the only one they were doing this to, and I began to wonder what was wrong with me. Why am I so different? How "bad" am I?

As a young kid, there was a constant aching on the inside because I couldn't measure up with my peers. The crushing blow that ripped every ounce of self-confidence out of me occurred in the fifth grade. The principle of our school taught our geography class. I remember him vividly. He was very tall and his black hair was slicked back with a smelly hair gel. He had a dark complexion, hairy arms and wore thick dark glasses. He was the most intimidating man I had ever encountered. Every Tuesday was test day and every week we were assigned new seats according to our test scores. That was one of the most painful experiences of my life. The first seat on the first row was for the highest score. One by one he called out the names and I found myself humiliated as each row filled up across the room and I was still standing. My name was the last one called and the walk to that seat in the back of the room was agonizing. It felt like I had been stripped naked and every eye was on me. It was humiliating – like someone screaming from the housetop, "That's the stupidest kid in the class!"

The entire year I went through that agonizing process week after week. It chipped away at my self-worth to the place where nothing was left. I began to close up and withdraw from everyone because I was so ashamed and embarrassed.

All throughout middle school, I would sit in a school counselor's office with my parents listening to their assessment of my lack of academic achievement. I vividly remember a comment from one counselor that haunted me for years. As he looked at my parents he said, "You need to understand he will never be college material. He will need to go to some kind of trade school. He will not be able to function in the business world." He said it again, "He will never be able to go to college." There is nothing more devastating than when someone puts you in a box by telling you what you will never do. His words were clear: I would never go to college, never have a good job, and never make good money. How I interpreted his assessment was that I might as well give up and not even try. So that's exactly what I did. His words did more than confine me to a "box" – it was more like nailing a coffin shut on any hope of a good life. A loss of confidence and insecurity became the raging battle that grew in me, and against what God had purposed for me to do in life.

There's no shortage of people who will tell you why you can't succeed in life. Think about how ridiculous it is that we allow someone to speak negatively into our lives and allow them to put limitations on us. Think about how often this happens. For instance, Angelina Jolie was a skinny nerd in high school who wore braces and glasses. The first time she auditioned for an acting role she was laughed at by the director and told to go home.

> *Think about how ridiculous it is that we allow someone to speak negatively into our lives and allow them to put limitations on us.*

New England Patriots quarterback Tom Brady, was second string on his high school football team and his coaches told him he was neither physically fit nor athletic enough to play at the college level.

Elvis Presley was told by a music teacher in high school that he was a terrible singer and that he should choose a different career.

Lucille Ball was sent home from acting school in New York because the teachers thought she was too shy and would never make it as an actress.

Walt Disney was fired by a newspaper editor because he lacked imagination.

Albert Einstein did not speak until he was four and struggled in learning to read, causing his teachers and parents to think he was mentally handicapped.

Thomas Edison was told by a teacher that he was "too stupid to learn anything."

When I was seventeen, I couldn't shake the feeling that God was calling me to full-time ministry. I continued to reject those thoughts as nothing but foolish fantasies, though I wanted it more than anything. I had a deep love and respect for God that had been instilled in me by my parents. I loved God, I loved the church, I loved ministry. But I also needed to go to college and receive a ministry degree. How could I? Those words still rang in my ears, "He will never go to college."

One night changed everything. On a Wednesday night I was sitting in our youth service with about thirty other students. I don't remember anything about the message that night but something had rattled me to the core. I knelt down in front of an old metal chair during a prayer time and started weeping. I didn't hear an audible voice but there might as well have been, because that night God made it clear that He was calling me to full-time ministry. I poured out every excuse I had and told God why I would fail and why it was impossible. Insecurity had already crippled me for the first part of my life. I had an extreme fear of public speaking. I must have cried a bucket of tears that night. When I stood up I felt like I had been scrubbed clean inside and out. It was the most refreshing thing I had ever experienced. It was like a weight had been removed from my shoulders. Something was rumbling on the inside that gave me courage to believe I could take on the world. It was like the God-given courage that David received to take on the lion, the bear, and Goliath. It was a total shift in thinking. The next day I told everybody that I was going to a Bible college and pursuing ministry.

What I found was that not too many people will share the same excitement in your dream as you. They are quick to inform you of all the obstacles that will stop your dream.

> *What I found was that not too many people will share the same excitement in your dream as you.*

Instead of listening to all the things people say, listen to what God has to say. The moment I stepped in the direction of God's plan, doors began to open. I went to college and I flourished – spiritually, socially and academically. It was like God opened my understanding on why I had such a difficult time learning. I always knew I had a creative mind and an overactive imagination. I was a visual learner. At the college level I discovered I could learn or memorize anything as long as I put it into story form. I began to do what everybody said I would never do.

So what about you? We all have our own story of why we can't. What's *your* personal nemesis? What is it that stops you from achieving those ridiculous dreams in the back of your mind?

Do I need to remind you that as a follower of Christ you have been transformed into a new creation?

> "Do not conform to the pattern of this world, but be transformed by the renewing of your mind. Then you will be able to test and approve what God's will is—his good, pleasing and perfect will." Romans 12:2 (NIV)

The Word of God moves you from living in the natural realm into the realm of the supernatural (this is the Kingdom of God being worked out on earth). You will never find the good, pleasing and perfect will of God that allows you to fulfill your God-given dream until you change your way of thinking. Human nature is to be negative, fearful and afraid of what others think. We don't advance because we are afraid of not measuring up.

Stage Jumpers

We all remember the shocking night of MTV's Video Music Awards when Taylor Swift came on stage to receive her trophy. Suddenly, Kanye came out of the audience, jumped on stage and interrupted Taylor's acceptance speech, declaring that Beyonce was the best and should have won. It was one of the most embarrassing moments on live television. Taylor stood there devastated, having been robbed of one of the greatest moments in her life. The gall of someone doing something like that is absolutely unthinkable.

Kanye doesn't have a say. It's not his award to give. His opinion doesn't count. In the same way, people will jump on your stage telling you why you can't and why you don't measure up.

Their opinion doesn't count. God's opinion is the only one that matters. Everything changes when we understand that we are nothing but empty, fragile vessels that the Creator of the universe now fills and uses to change the nations. All we have to do is stop looking at our weaknesses and recognize His strength.

Your dream is God-given! Your dream has not passed you by. Remember, be an AVID dreamer and it will manifest. God wants you to get your hopes up!

"Now faith is confidence in what we hope for and assurance about what we do not see." Hebrews 11:1 (NIV)

The definition of hope is "confident expectation." You need to be confident in your dream. This is the very reason why scripture tells us that it is impossible to please God without faith – faith believing God is big enough to see your dream through. God doesn't just want you to dream, he wants you to live the dream!

John Gardner, advisor to four U.S. Presidents, often said, "What we have before us are some breathtaking opportunities disguised as insoluble problems."

Challenge causes you to come face to face with yourself. It reminds you of what's important, what you value, and where you want to go. Every time I find myself surrounded by insurmountable odds, and I start down the path of stress and worry, I literally make myself stop dead in my tracks. I continue through the process of self-talk. I start to talk myself off the ledge of despair. When I hit nothing but brick walls is when I declare God's Word. This challenge is nothing more than an opportunity to advance to the next level.

Do you remember the story of the computer science professor Randy Pausch, who delivered his last lecture at Carnegie Mellon University? Randy was dying of pancreatic cancer. That day he said, "The brick walls are there for a reason. They're not there to keep us out. The brick walls are there to give us a chance to show how badly we want something."

I watched his speech on television along with much of the world. It was riveting knowing that he faced death within a few days. What inspired me was when he said, "Brick walls are simply doors to a new future." He asked, "How badly do you want it?"

Whether the challenge is large or small, *leaders* take charge of their future. Casting vision and leading people through the vision are two very different processes. I spent months doing nothing but casting vision. Casting vision is the ability to inspire, educate and motivate people to see what they've never seen before. The next step isn't so easy – leading through the vision.

Chapter 8

The Elimination Challenge

In an attempt to keep things moving forward I decided to have another meeting with all of my staff. I scheduled an all-day vision-casting meeting at a hotel downtown. We desperately needed to wrap our heads around this new direction and get everything detailed out. Again, this young staff began expressing their belief that we were too slow in making decisions. What I thought was warp-speed they saw as moving at a turtle's pace. They weren't satisfied with progress that was just inching along. That morning they had their guns loaded and opened up in verbal rapid-fire.

It was just one of those days. I wanted to pull out a roll of duct tape and tape their mouths shut. They had way too much to say. They wanted me to be a little more reckless in just throwing crazy ideas out to the congregation, with no idea how it would happen or where we would get the money. "We need to cast a vision so big that we don't have a clue how it's going to happen." My response being, "Do what? You've got to be kidding." Well, the reason why this discussion came up was because I was always saying to them, "Before you start something make sure you have all your ducks in a row." Sitting around that table, in a way, they were making fun of my ideology of having everything fail-proof. In their minds, we were way too practical and methodical and playing it too safe. Their question was, "Where is our faith that God will do the impossible? When we launch out in some new direction, we always have to have everything fail-proof before presenting it to the church. It seems like we are doing everything in our own strength." Well, the argument fired up and I proceeded to tell them the importance of planning, mapping, and strategizing before presenting a big idea to the congregation. I said emphatically, "I expect us to always have our ducks in a row and have everything detailed out." There was a lot of wisdom in what I was saying but the more I talked, the more I realized I was greatly limiting our advancement. I had never really thought about it before but I was trying hard to ensure success by my own human abilities and plans. To a large degree, I was eliminating the supernatural out of the equation – although there was not a chance I was going to admit that in front of *them*!

By nature I want to be in control of my surroundings and leave no room for failure – succeed at all costs. I then realized that with this mentality we would only advance as far as our human abilities would take us. What was my biggest obstacle? Failure. I hate failure. But is failure really all that bad? How is failure defined? It means to miss the mark and to fall short of expectations. According to that definition, there is a 100 percent failure rate in almost everything we do. You can't eliminate failure from your life. The real question we need to be asking is, "What will I do when I fail in ministry, business, school, or in my own personal goals?" We all have heard this a million times and yet we just can't accept it as truth: "Failures are stepping-stones."

I personally don't like that idea, but it really is the truth. It's the process of learning and growing.

Here are three ways to look at failure from a different perspective.

1. Failures are just stepping-stones.

We overemphasize it. We make the mistake of seeing our failure as the final result. Failure is a part of a larger process of learning and growing. Take time to analyze successful people and you will notice that they have developed a unique mindset. They realize that failure is an integral part of success. Failure is just the realization that there is a better way of achieving your goal. Don't make the mistake of seeing failure as an isolated event, but see it as a part of the process. Failure is

> *Failure is only the end if you allow it to stop you.*

125

only the end if you allow it to stop you. It's a stepping-stone that brings you closer to your goal.

2. Failing is part of innovation.

"I have not failed. I've just found 10,000 ways that won't work."
– Thomas Edison

There is a big difference between creative people and innovators. A creative team can come up with all kinds of ideas, but it's the innovators who have the courage to go and make it happen. Guess what happens when they do? They fail many times but it gives them the ability to improve their approach.

3. Everybody is afraid.

"Courage is not the absence of fear, but rather the judgment that something else is more important than fear." – Ambrose Redmoon

Fear will always be a part of the process. As we read through the Bible you will find, in every major story, fear and faith as the central theme. They always work side by side and one always wins.

Fear is the opposite of who God is.

> "For God gave us a spirit not of fear but of power and love and self-control." 1 Timothy 1:7(ESV)

Achievers succeed not because they're not afraid, they achieve because they overcome fear through confidence in our great God!

While sitting at a table during that all-day meeting with my young staff, I was intrigued by their child-like faith. In their eyes, nothing seemed impossible. In some ways it was wild, reckless faith. I remembered years ago when I had that same wild spirit. When you're around it, it's refreshing and empowering. It was something I had lost throughout the years. I have personally always leaned to the side of being a perfectionist. I want to hit the bull's eye every time. How ridiculous is that? If I'm able to hit perfection every time, then do you know what that means? I've set the target too close. I need to move the target far enough away that I can't even hit it. I need to keep shooting until my skills eventually improve to the place that I'm able to hit the target again and then again. Then it's time to move the target back. When I looked at it this way I realized that failure is my best friend. Failure leads to mastery. I knew it was time to start aiming at some things I never believed I could hit.

Facing the Giant of an Old Philosophy

I certainly had big hopes for the future, but I was also facing a giant that is not easily conquered. This was the giant of an old, long-standing church philosophy. We had an established church that was completely centered on ministering to the already saved. What I began to realize was that we were still following a church schedule and programs that were implemented seventy-five years ago. We had the traditional Sunday school, Sunday morning worship service, Sunday evening service, Wednesday night service, Wednesday night children's programs, plus all the other ministries that had been added throughout the years.

In a seventy-five-year-old church, the schedule and programs were as sacred as the Virgin Mary in the Catholic Church. I found myself barely staying afloat, preparing for one service after another. With that many sermons to prepare, I had no time for vision casting or pouring into staff members. That kind of schedule will throw you into a day-to-day cycle of simply maintaining. Church services were rolling around so fast that there was very little thought going into them. That means nothing was functioning at a high level of excellence. I had to ask myself the question, "Why are we still following a schedule set by the leadership back in the forties?" It makes no sense. People's lives and needs are far different today than they were years ago. If I were starting a church, what would be the ideal structure? The crazy thought came to me, "What if we eliminated all ministries and completely started over again?" I'm talking about church services, Bible studies, men's and women's ministries, children's programs...everything. I was literally thinking of eliminating all volunteer leadership across the board. Can this really happen in an established, traditional church? Would people really be willing to let go of ministries they've been leading for many years? If you've been involved in church for very long, then you know how protective people become of their ministry. They have done it for so long that they take on ownership. The danger of this is that they see themselves as the ultimate authority and no one has the right to tell them what to do. Most ministry leaders believe the ministry they are leading is the most important in the church. They have become so entrenched with and passionate about their ministry that they are not going to let anyone threaten the existence of that program – even if it has floundered for years. It's their baby and, even if it's an ugly baby, they are going to hold on tight and protect it to the end.

In many situations they will even see the pastoral staff as the enemy and take on an "us" against "them" mentality. This becomes so strong that they will defy church vision and leadership by not following proper protocol. This is how power struggles develop that can destroy the effectiveness of the church. Many times people forget, or they are not aware of the strong scriptural teaching on the principles of God-ordained authority.

The Bible is very clear on the subject of submission to authority, not just in the church, but also for husbands, wives, children, employees, parents, and spiritual authority.

As I read through the Bible I see a few words that are synonymous with submission: honor, respect, giving, love, and humility.

Find a person who understands submission to authority and you'll see a person who is humble, full of love, unselfish, accountable, and personally responsible. Find a person who does not understand submission to authority and you'll see a person who is prideful, full of criticism, selfish, self-ruled, and spiritually irresponsible.

We who are parents all know how important it is for our kids to obey and follow our instructions. Yet we all have more than a little trouble honoring the authority that is over our own lives. That's a blatant double standard. The truth is, God has placed an entire network of people in this world into positions of authority. I'm not just referring to our government leaders but also to the leaders in our workplaces and in our families.

Coming under authority and showing respect isn't easy. Nobody wants to be told what to do or how to do it. We criticize anybody who makes a decision we don't like. It's not right. It's not fair. It's not good for *me*.

In our country, we've taken our right to free speech to unbelievable levels. We openly criticize our leaders, our country, and pretty much anything else that doesn't line up with what we want. We don't see anything wrong with belittling those who are in authority over us. Spiritually, this is a serious offense and we rarely think about the consequences of our words and actions.

When we usurp authority, God's protection and favor are lifted from us. The bottom line is that God expects us to respect Him and His choices. He expects that we will respect the people he's placed in authority over us. That doesn't mean you have to agree with every one of their decisions. But it does mean we still need to show respect for the position and the person who is in that position.

> *When we usurp authority, God's protection and favor are lifted from us.*

Look at the strong warning Paul gives us about submitting to authority:

> "Let everyone be subject to the governing authorities, for there is no authority except that which God has established. The authorities that exist have been established by God. Consequently, whoever rebels against the authority is rebelling against what God has instituted, and those who do so will bring judgment on themselves." Romans 13:1-2 (NIV)

Don't participate in backbiting, gossiping, or criticizing your bosses or others in authority. There is nothing wrong with having constructive conversations, but there is a fine line between offering our opinion and becoming disrespectful.

There are times when decisions will negatively impact us. But just remember that how we react to these moments will determine God's favor or judgment upon our lives. There is no magic pill that can make you feel good about having to submit to authority. But know that when we make the conscious effort to submit to the authority, we have put God first. Regardless of how it feels, you are planting seeds that will produce a harvest of blessing in your life.

Over and over, the Bible establishes the structure of authority. In the local church there is a shepherd and the sheep. The sheep don't lead the flock. The sheep don't tell the shepherd on which hill they want to graze. The shepherd is put in a position to lead and protect. If God has placed you in a leadership role, there is high accountability placed in your hands to lead in a godly manner and not cower to the pleas or demands of all people.

I heard someone say something at a conference that absolutely turned my leadership around. It was so simple and yet so profound. "Leaders don't lead people where they *want* to go, but leaders lead people where they *need* to go." Authority and leadership have been established and put in place by God himself.

It's an absolute to keep things in order. For instance, kids follow the lead of their parents. Students follow the lead of their teachers. Military personnel follow the lead of their superior officers. It is apparent that at any level, when authority is usurped, it will jeopardize order, success, and advancement. Our world is in such desperate need of spiritual leadership. There are too many spiritual leaders today who are satisfied with just maintaining and see themselves as being in more of a popularity contest than as a strong leader having to make the hard decisions. They might be more interested in a good salary and a secure future than in making waves. It's easy to lose sight of the big picture. We must never forget that we are dealing with the eternal souls of people.

Pondering the idea of dismantling a long-existing yet ineffective ideology was completely overwhelming to me. I sat down with a few staff members, pitched the idea and told them that the first elimination I was targeting was Sunday night services.

The important thing to remember is that we were not eliminating things for the sake of elimination. We must remember why we are making the elimination. My reasoning was that if we could consolidate all of our resources, talent and energy into one service instead of three completely different services – Sunday morning, Sunday night and Wednesday night – we could make a stronger impact. Instead of three similar services that specifically catered to believers, we could now go to one very creative service that would speak the language of the unsaved.

This would enable our worship team to perfect their worship set. They would have more time to research the newest and most up-to-date songs that relate to a younger generation and they would have the time to work on cover songs that set the scene for the theme of the day. All kinds of creative aspects could be developed to enhance the worship experience.

Our staff seemed very excited about the possible change so I immediately scheduled a board meeting to inform them that we were going to cancel Sunday night services. That night in the board meeting I was immediately confronted with strong opposition. One particular board member was adamant that it was wrong and he would never be in favor. I could tell this was going in the wrong direction so I tabled the conversation quickly and moved on to another topic.

The next day at the office, I told my personal assistant that I wanted her to sit in the back of the auditorium each Sunday night and take attendance for the next three months. I wanted to know who was actually committed to those services. The board member, who was so adamant about keeping Sunday night services, had an average attendance of about once a month. He didn't even value it enough to come every week but wanted everybody else to pour time and energy into those services so that if he did want to come it was there for his enjoyment. This is the reason leaders cannot be held hostage by the opinions of every person. Many times, opinions will center on personal preference instead of the overall good of the church.

In a board meeting several months later I addressed the issue again, explaining in much detail why I wanted to eliminate ministries. Under the current leadership and structure these ministries were not producing. I made sure that everyone understood we were going to narrow our focus to only a few things, but we were going to do them with excellence. I laid the attendance records out on the table, showing them who was coming and how poorly Sunday night was being attended. The attendance records silenced the board member who seemed to be so against the elimination.

Thorough Communication

One morning I walked into the office and asked my assistant to divide up the entire adult congregation into small groups of ten to fifteen people. I wanted an intimate setting in a home with coffee and dessert. She organized the event with host families opening up their homes and providing desserts and drinks. She scheduled me for sixteen straight nights. Each night I would sit with wonderful people, sharing our new vision of reaching a young generation.

All sixteen nights I had a young college student join me. Each night he shared how he had never been in a church outside of attending a funeral service and how he had been a professed atheist who had written off God and religion as nonsense.

Then, on the campus of the University of New Mexico, someone invited him to church. He was very reluctant but finally came. The first day that he had ever experienced a church service he became so completely overwhelmed that he could hardly get through it. When I gave the invitation for those who wanted to receive Christ into their lives he walked to the front and dropped to his knees weeping. He was a mess. Now, just a few months later, he's serving in our church almost every night of the week. He also was solely responsible for a little over twenty new college students now attending our church who were also very involved. Each night when he had finished and sat down, I told the group gathered that he was a direct product of our decision to reach a young generation. I continued telling them that there were thousands out there just like him. All they need is an invitation and for us to stand ready to open up our arms and receive them. Those nights were electrifying.

I asked them to trust me. I wanted to take them on the greatest spiritual journey that they could ever imagine. Together we were going to lead hundreds and even thousands to Christ over the next few years. I explained why we needed a change. We weren't growing and were just barely maintaining. I explained that the quality of our ministry was subpar. I could see some ministry leaders bristle up – being offended that I would suggest that they weren't leading well. I continued to talk about how many of our ministries no longer aligned with our new vision. I told them that we needed to eliminate much of our current schedule to focus all of our time and energy on a few things until we made them exceptional. In every meeting the same question came up: "Pastor, how many ministries are you going to eliminate?" All sixteen nights, at that moment, I felt like I had a mouthful of cotton and I struggled getting the words out. When the words came, it sounded like I said, "All but Sunday Morning service and Wednesday night student ministries."

"Pastor, could you repeat that? I think I heard you wrong!" Well, they didn't hear it wrong...and that was the plan. I talked from my heart, telling them that I knew it would be painful at times but that together we could do something great for God's Kingdom. "I want you to look at this like we are starting all over again. This is like planting a new church. This can be one of the most thrilling experiences of your life." Each night we all stood and prayed together that God would lead every step of this new endeavor. Looking around the room it was certainly not difficult to know who was with me and who was not.

Time for Radical Measures

Within the next year and a half we had dissolved Sunday night services, Sunday school, Wednesday evening services, men's and women's ministries and a children's ministry on Wednesday nights. We had taken our operation down to bare bones.

This was an extremely painful process but it was absolutely impossible to move forward with the seventy-five-year-old church model that had been stale for the past twenty years.

On cigarette packaging there is a strong warning of health risks associated with smoking that can led to death. Let me give a strong warning when it comes to church program elimination. It's a process that can be very dangerous to your well-being. There were a couple of times I thought I was going to lose my life when meeting with ministry leaders and informing them we were phasing out their ministry. This is definitely not the way to go unless you have exhausted every other option.

There may be different times in our lives when we need major, life-saving surgery, while other times we may just need a minor procedure to get us back to full health. As a church, our only option was radical surgery in hopes of getting us out of the spiritual deathbed. So we made the necessary cuts and endured the pain of recovery. Over a period of about eighteen months we had eliminated almost everything but Sunday morning services and student ministries.

This may sound a bit radical, but if the death-grip of dead religion has taken hold of your local church, maybe we should follow Christ's lead and do something radical – like fashioning a whip out of cords and driving out those who are blocking the advancement of the church. That sounds really harsh, doesn't it? I've never known anybody who has ever done that except Jesus. But maybe no one has ever been as serious about the church as He was. Maybe we've forgotten the urgency of our mission as His Church.

The other thing we must always remember as leaders is that we are called to love people as much as we love ourselves, which is an extremely high calling. Shepherds love their sheep to the point of risking their lives for them. Leading a church is absolute warfare. As the leader of the local church you will have to make many unpopular decisions. We've never been called to be politically correct or to be afraid of offending people because we're not leading in a way that they prefer. The church is the hope of the world and if we believe that, then we can't afford failure. If the church we are leading is not reaching the lost, then we as leaders need to take the bull by the horns and do what it takes to see that the church fulfills its purpose.

David Livingstone once said,

> "I will go anywhere, provided it be forward."

What great advice. As leaders we must always be moving forward. Never retreating, regressing or stagnating. When we retreat, we are running away. When regressing, we are drifting backward. When stagnating, we are staying in one place.

Look at what Jesus said:

> "And from the time John the Baptist began preaching until now, the Kingdom of Heaven has been forcefully advancing, and violent people are attacking it."
> Matthew 11:12 (NLT)

The kingdom of God advances by men and women determined to move it forward even when met by violent resistance.

The reason for breaking everything down to ground level is to create a church environment that turns its eyes upon the world's needs. In other words, to forcefully advance the Kingdom of God. As we intently evaluated everything we were doing, surprisingly we found that most of our church busyness was centered on biblical self-consumption and not on a hurting and lost world. We were an internally-focused church and not an externally-focused church – operating completely opposite of Christ's teaching. Remember what Christ said, "For the Son of Man came to seek and to save what was lost."

For many years our church people spent so many hours a week on just attending church services and Bible studies that it left them with no time to influence and impact the world we are called to reach. What I began to understand is that you can't change your church culture until you first change your church philosophy. This is what I had missed for many years. There has to be a very clear vision of *who* you are and *what* you're trying to accomplish. For so long I would attend conferences and try to glean from progressive churches, desperately trying to implement ideas that would create church

> *What I began to understand is that you can't change your church culture until you first change your church philosophy.*

growth. New ideas like stage lighting, new worship songs, a creative service element, and small group models. We also noticed that casual dress had become the new trend. We would come back from a conference and decide that we're going to start wearing designer jeans instead of coats and ties. It was all in great hopes that if we did what successful churches were doing, we would experience the same success. Ideas are beneficial, but monumental change will never take place until we take our church through a philosophical change – bringing them to a place where there is a *why* behind everything we do.

I could have asked any old timer in our church the question, "What's the purpose of the church?" There is not a doubt in my mind that they would say, "The Great Commission. Winning souls." The truth was, our structure did not support that. Nothing we did was designed to win the lost. It was designed to keep the saved. When I finally understood the difference between just copying some good church ideas versus creating a philosophical change we began to see transformation as a church. When I clearly communicated that we were going to be a church of all ages committed to reaching a young generation, I had made clear our purpose, and purpose defines the bull's eye of our target and the filter through which our decisions are made.

Over a period of decades we had slipped into the trap of self-focused Christianity. Our philosophical change was to cause people to think, "Who am I pouring into?" We needed children and student ministries that weren't focused on doing ministry *for* kids but doing ministry *through* kids. We needed a worship experience that attracts and speaks to the young and lost.

It was a philosophy that causes parents and grandparents to say, "We've had our day, now it's their turn." Eliminating programs and ministries was still very challenging but at least people could see where we were going. We were rebuilding to reach a young, lost generation. Still there was resistance from many people who were not sold on this new focus. For these long-time church leaders, the thought of letting go of their ministries was more than they could handle. It was their ministry, their identity, and without it they felt lost. And I agonized for them. As I sat down with these leaders, I assured them that I understood what they were feeling because I was going through the same process myself. When we had completed the elimination you could sense how all of our volunteers seemed totally lost. They were used to spending so much time at the church and now they had no responsibilities and nothing to do. For me, this was the scariest moment of all. Everything seemed so unstable and disconnected, and I wondered how long we could hold this together without a mass exit.

I used our Sunday morning service as an opportunity to motivate and encourage these leaders and to convey to them that something great was about to happen! Every day I was on my knees praying, "God, something great better happen or I'm in deep trouble."

It was now the end of May and school was about to be out for the summer. One of the ways I communicated the positive side of the elimination process was through the Old Testament teaching on the sabbatical rest.

I spoke several weeks on how we were going to take a three month sabbatical from our church labor. After seventy-five years it was now time to let the field rest. I wanted all of our leaders and volunteers to take the summer off. This was going to be a season of rest.

I taught from Leviticus 25 on the sabbatical rest and also from Acts where the disciples were told to "wait" – to not go out and do ministry but wait until the coming of the Holy Spirit. There is a purpose in waiting and a reason for resting. One of the things we were doing was allowing enough time to pass so that old ministry programs could die a true death.

I encouraged them not to become restless but to use this time for self-reflection and to center on family members and one another. This way of thinking seemed to bring a bit of ease to the situation. I talked to everyone about how exciting it was to be on the ground level of building a new vision to change the next generation. We love our sons and daughters and grandchildren so much that we are willing to walk through a transition even if it proves to be difficult at times.

After eighteen months of small group meetings, confrontations, board meetings, high levels of tension, frustration, and yes, people leaving the church, we were set to raise up a young generation.

Chapter 9

The Power of Narrowed Focus

As a result of having eliminated almost every ministry in the church, we had now primarily narrowed our focus to weekend services. I knew that our weekend services would be the bridge that would connect us to the spiritually lost in our city. That meant we had to rethink everything we had been doing for decades. The big question in my mind was, how does a church full of churched people attract unchurched people? The first step in this endeavor was to implement a creative team that could help us accomplish this task. For days I thought through a host of people, jotting down names of possible team members. I ended up choosing three staff members and three volunteers as a team of people who would be responsible for designing the most engaging and exciting worship experiences possible. I can still remember how excited I was for our first meeting. Our building was so run down and depressing that I took one of our classrooms upstairs and asked a couple of ladies in the church to remodel it with paint, wall hangings, a couch, and chairs. When they finished, it was the nicest room in the church. This would be our new creative room. I wanted the best environment to stimulate our creativity. It was going to be incredible. Ideas would be flying from every direction. Well, our first meeting wasn't anything like I had envisioned. We all just sat there totally blank. Every idea was based off of something we had already done in the past. Every idea seemed to fall flat and go nowhere. Coming up with new ideas was like pulling teeth. I found myself frustrated with their lack of creativity. I certainly didn't have any earth shattering ideas myself, but after all, that's the reason they were there. The positive, upbeat, fun meeting that I had envisioned had turned to a negative, argumentative, and depressing one.

Each time we started down a train of thought it was interrupted by a couple of team members who seemed to find a reason why every idea wouldn't work. I quickly realized this was not the team that was going to take us to another level. It became very clear to me that building an effective creative team was going to be a long process. Probably more important than anything else, this group had to have chemistry with one another. We kept rotating people on and off this team until finally, after a year, we had developed the right group of people. This group became the driving force behind every change we made.

For a team of this nature to function properly there has to be great trust and respect. The other crucial element is that there must be extreme confidence between this team and the senior pastor. In many ways they will be creating the environment and setting the culture for the entire church. This is the reason why the church vision cannot be fluid. It has to be set in concrete so that there is no room for any misguided direction. Everyone involved must know the vision, be able to quote the vision, and understand that we live and die by the vision. At this stage of the game I knew without a doubt where we were going. I took a strong lead in all the decisions and planning during the beginning stages of this team. The problem with that is although we are leading the transformation of cultural change, our decision making in a creative planning session is often jaded by the fact that all complaints, issues, and disturbances are going to end up on our desk. When people are upset and mad they aren't angry at other staff members or volunteer leaders. They are angry at the one in charge.

We are all very aware of the old saying, "The buck stops here." It was U.S. President Harry S. Truman who made this statement famous. He had a sign with this inscription on his desk. This was meant to indicate that he didn't "pass the buck" to anyone else but accepted personal responsibility for the way the country was governed. This same sense of responsibility is what causes many leaders to stop, pause, back up, and be too cautious instead of staying the

We're not so sure we want to deal with the consequences of rocking the boat.

course. We're not so sure we want to deal with the consequences of rocking the boat.

Even though I was 100 percent sure of the direction we were going, I still found myself wavering when influential people began to raise concerns regarding our new direction.

> "Write the vision clearly on tablets so that the person who reads it can run and tell other people." Habakkuk 2:2 (ERV)

After all these years the one thing I fully understood is that you can never go wrong by following the advice of God's Word.

So, I scheduled a weekend getaway for our staff in a beautiful, quaint lodge in Ruidoso, New Mexico. Those three days proved to have the greatest impact of anything we had ever done.

That Monday morning we sat on the deck overlooking the Lincoln National Forest. This was the place where everything changed. We sat in front of a white board, and the first question I asked was, "Why do we exist as a church? Not the church in general, but as an individual church. What's our unique DNA?" Everyone there that day had a good idea of who we were and who we wanted to be. There was something so empowering about seeing it unfold before our eyes. As we continued working through this process, we wrote out our direction, vision, and core values. After nine straight hours of hard labor we had accomplished our task.

That evening, as I looked around the room, I could tell everyone was mentally exhausted, but there was such a sense of accomplishment. These were not mere words but now the path that paved the way to our new destination. Not one of us understood the tremendous impact this was going to have on our church.

The next month I launched a nine-week teaching series on our new core values. For our church, it was like a light switched on. With extreme clarity everyone could now see into our future. It was the game plan to fulfill our God-given calling. No longer would we fall into the category of a floundering church. Now we had a game plan to fulfill our kingdom agenda with excellence – which is always the foundation to success.

Perfect Record

Many years ago there was an NFL team who found themselves in last place. The owner had been frustrated over the past few years because of their losing record. They had gone through several head coaches in a short amount of time and yet nothing changed. In 1970, the owner of this football team hired another head coach in hopes of turning this losing streak around. The young new coach arrived and walked into the room to meet the players for the first time. This team meeting would be one they would never forget. He stood before them with his arms folded and was completely silent. Without saying a word he just stared at them. Silently, he scanned the crowd, making eye contact with each player. This went on for what seemed to be an eternity. It became extremely awkward and uncomfortable. Several veteran players lowered their heads to keep from laughing. Then, finally, the coach spoke in a clear and convincing voice: "Men, we are going to be champions in the NFL."

Almost every player in there was thinking, "Who does he think he is? How many times have we already heard those same words from previous coaches? Who does he think he's talking to? We are the worst team in the league." He then continued, "The reason why I say that is because I have a plan of action that will work." That coach was Don Shula with the Miami Dolphins, who led the team to two straight Super Bowls. They were the best in the NFL. This story can be related to every aspect of life. The key to being successful is to have a plan. We now had a plan that was going to work.

Leader, Listen Well!

We were now nearing the Christmas season, and we were planning to make the Christmas Eve service the best event in the city. The goal was to attract the unchurched. As we sat in a planning meeting an idea came up to implement a ballet element into the service. I immediately said no. Now, remember, we were coming from a very conservative church culture. My response was, "We will offend so many people in our church by having a dance. That's not going to happen, and it's not going to work. Next idea." I silenced the group and now they all just sat there. It was like I had thrown cold water on their creative fire. After what seemed like an eternity, our worship pastor broke the silence and asked, "Is a ballet a sinful act? If the dress attire is very modest and tasteful, is a ballet something sinful?" He continued on, "Pastor, you are constantly saying from the platform that when we plan our weekend services, we are planning them with your unsaved friends in mind. Tell us again, who are we trying to reach? If we are a church of all ages committed to reaching a young and lost generation, then are we trying to speak and relate to the unchurched or not? If something is not sinful or immoral, then why are we afraid? We are going right back to our old ways and doing what you said we would never do again, be controlled by a religious mindset. The very mindset that held this church captive for over fifty years." Wow. As I sat there I had to ask myself, "Am I being driven by fear or by vision?"

So I backed up and said, "Alright, let's talk about it and detail it out to see what it would look like." On opening night of our Christmas services I literally made myself sick from being so worried about church people getting upset about a dance in the church. Well, we went for it and it turned out to be one of the most beautiful and powerful elements we had ever done. The young girl who performed the dance was one of the star students at a Christian dance studio here in town. It was extremely beautiful, powerful and professional. It opened up the door to work with many other students from that studio. As a result, many of their parents started visiting and are now faithfully attending our church. It was a wealth of talent that helped us to implement many aspects of the arts into our weekend services with a higher level of excellence. Using many elements of the arts in our services started attracting other gifted people in the arts who wanted to use their talents for the Lord, but had never been given the opportunity in the church.

We began to look at the worship experience in a whole new way. It is no longer like it was in my early days of pastoring. Churches were primarily a duel event – worship and preaching – with very little thought given to anything else. Church today has become a corporate event. We are creating a service experience that draws every aspect to a central theme from the time people walk through the doors of our building to the time they leave. The more time, creativity, and organization we implement into our services, the more I feel we are honoring our creative and organized God.

There was a powerful yet false belief system I had fallen prey to that had deceived me for years. It was the belief that being overly scheduled or structured in our services meant that you were not leaving room for the Holy Spirit to move and work. The mentality was that the Holy Spirit only works on the spur of the moment.

Let me share with you the power of a well-planned creative structure. There is a couple in our church who owns a small business. It was just an ordinary day at work when one of their customers walked in, who they had known for many years. The owners were carrying on a conversation with this gentleman when they reached out and handed him an invitation card to our church. They told him that they would love for him to join them for service that upcoming Sunday, which happened to be Easter. They asked him to be their guest and to sit with them. He graciously accepted the invitation and walked out the door.

As the week passed and the weekend was nearing, the gentleman became nervous, not really knowing what to expect. It had been almost thirty years since he had been in church. Being home alone in the evenings, he had a lot of time to think about the commitment he had made to attend our service that Easter. His mind rushed back to when he was a young man attending church. There was an old hymn that came to mind that he had not thought of in years: Nothing But The Blood Of Jesus. It kept running over and over in his mind. Easter morning he dressed and nervously drove to church. He found his seat with his friends, the lights faded down, and at center stage was a grand piano, dimly lit. Our worship pastor began singing Nothing But The Blood of Jesus. The man was so overwhelmed with emotion that he burst out in tears and said, "Dear God, I'm home. I'm finally home." He looked up and said, "Jesus, I love you and I need you," and Christ entered his life at that very moment. Since that day he has said many times, "I've never been the same from that moment."

Now this is what I want you to see. Months before, on a Sunday evening, we had invited the creative team to our home to begin planning our Easter service. As we were brainstorming, someone said, "You know, for a long time we have been starting our services off with a high energy worship song. How about doing something completely different, maybe something unexpected like an old hymn? The opening number will start with a video of our worship pastor playing a piano in an old country church. Then we will transition live on stage with him playing a grand piano at center stage." Someone said, "I know it may be a crazy idea, but let's go old-school." Immediately, it struck a chord with all of us. Someone else said, "What old song should we sing?" Several titles were suggested and then our worship pastor, Jonathan, said, "How about Nothing But The Blood of Jesus?"

Unanimously, we agreed. Sitting in our living room, no one realized the power nor the presence of the Holy Spirit that was at work, directing us months in advance to set up one man's life-changing day.

Quickly we began to see our weekend services take on a whole new dimension of excellence. The old saying, two heads are better than one, is very true. The enormous power of six people, sitting in a room, asking the question, "How can we convey the message of God's Word more effectively," had greatly enhanced the spiritual impact on those who attended our services.

Spiritual growth was automatically producing numerical growth. I knew we had to prepare for greater numbers of people and also be able to sustain that growth. I remember sharing with them something I heard at the C3 Conference in Dallas: "If you are a church of one hundred, then you need to structure and organize like you're a church of five hundred. If you are a church of five hundred, then act like a church of a thousand." That should just be common sense. I had never gone as far as learning from leaders of larger churches and structuring our organization at their level – things such as bylaws, procedures, staffing, vision, philosophy and finances.

As a church staff we began to call larger churches that were accomplishing things we wanted to accomplish. We identified churches that had mastered certain fields of ministry that we wanted to emulate. I knew the fastest way to make changes was to simply do what others had already mastered. We started sending staff members and teams of volunteers to larger churches and scheduled meetings with their staff members to observe their ministries. We found that everyone was extremely helpful and went the second mile to assist us. We sent people to Fellowship Church to sit down with their media team and to understand their creative process. We sent others to observe the college ministry at New Life Church in Colorado Springs, CO. We sent staff members to Andy Stanley's North Point Church, to observe multiple services. Our guest services team went to The Potter's House in Dallas. We also set up phone conferences with staff members across the country to pick their brains. We learned and copied everything we could to help us think differently and on a larger scale.

Isaac Newton once said, "If I have seen further than others, it is by standing upon the shoulders of giants." I want to seek out the giants of our day to learn what they already know.

Excuses Kill Your Future

My wife, Kay, took the lead on our creative team and was responsible for setting up the structure that would take us to another level in creativity. Unknowingly, at the time, the main thing that needed to change was our approach to new ideas. We had to remove the excuses we had used explaining why we couldn't do what larger churches were doing. See if these "growth-excuses" sound familiar:

"Adding creative elements are just too expensive."

"There aren't enough creative people in our church."

"People aren't willing to give that much time to the church."

"We don't have enough full-time staff members."

"We live in a resort town."

"We don't live in the Bible belt."

"We don't have the money big churches have."

"Our facilities limit our ability for growth."

"Our church is not in a good location."

At different times I've used each of these excuses. I saw this played out firsthand when I attended a ministers' roundtable in our city. We spent six hours together talking about leadership, finances, and church growth. A large church was hosting the event and in attendance were primarily pastors of small churches. Everyone was hoping to take away valuable information that would make positive changes in their own churches. When it was over, my son Dustin got in the car and said, "Did you notice that almost every pastor verbalized excuses why they could not grow? It seemed like everyone there had that one obstacle that became their excuse for making growth impossible."

Think about how easy it is and also how ridiculous it is to allow our thought process to go down this path. In reality, that is a weak way of thinking. We often believe that even though God has called us to the ministry, and to a particular congregation, we will experience nothing but failure, and we live as though we believe that there are obstacles God Himself is unable to overcome. We can never allow circumstances to dictate our perspective of God's power.

Remember, the person who really wants to do something finds a way. The other person finds an excuse. Benjamin Franklin once said, "He that is good for making excuses is seldom good for anything else." Excuses will destroy your destiny.

> *the person who really wants to do something finds a way. The other person finds an excuse.*

No matter what the reason for church stagnation, leaders have to realize that connecting, motivating, and leading are too important for us to allow any excuse to stand in the way.

It's important to "keep the main thing the main thing." Mostly, the weekend services are where our vision comes to life and the place where a visitor forms their first impression of our church and the God that we represent.

Prepare Today For Who You Want To Be

We took seriously the fact that we were designing everything to sustain a future attendance of a thousand people. So, we started putting into place structures and positions that were so overkill for our size of church that it was really embarrassing. We didn't care. We were on a mission. And we were putting all of our eggs in one basket. I was calling an end to our church sabbatical and now it was time for everyone to find a place to serve…and I meant everyone. We were creating as many volunteer opportunities as possible. This was a culture change and everyone had to join in. This is how we did it…

We detailed out as many job descriptions as possible – from the top of our structure to the bottom. I started with myself by forming a teaching team. That was certainly a foreign concept to me and completely out of my comfort zone. It seemed like more trouble than it was worth. I didn't need someone telling me what and how to preach. Why did I need input on writing my sermons? Well, we did it anyway because that's what large and successful churches were doing, and admittedly these Pastors were better communicators than I. So I decided that if they did it, I would do it.

Below you will find some of the things we put in place that may seem so elementary, yet created an avalanche of change and growth for me, and I know it can do the same for you.

Teaching Team:

The purpose of this team is to brainstorm and develop future sermon series. They assist in providing scriptural insight, creative illustrations, quotes, or anything that will enhance the message for the weekend.

This team consists of myself (Lead Pastor) and a few key staff members. The size of this team is from three to five people. We schedule an all-day meeting once a year for annual planning – usually in October. Various themes become staples for the following year such as Family, Marriage, Spiritual Emphasis, Vision, annual conferences, etc. The goal is not to create working titles but general themes. This team will also meet once a week detailing the titles and direction of the series – including titles for individual sermons.

This team should work about two months in advance. This is necessary to help the creative team in planning service elements and for designing the graphics and branding for the series.

They also will take time in the beginning of each meeting to critique the previous sermon. This is where I listen to their input and give them the liberty to speak honestly about the weaknesses and strengths of my messages and delivery. At times it was extremely difficult to not be defensive or stubborn and simply ignore their advice. Now what I have found is that it is imperative to have other voices speaking into my life. They see things that I would never pick up on, and they speak into my life from a totally different perspective. Here are a few of the things they talked to me about: I have to stop using a preacher's voice while speaking. They encouraged me to be more conversational, to tell more personal stories and to be a little more transparent. They believed my sermons were too structured and not engaging enough. Believe me, this was hard to swallow at times. However, if you can swallow your pride and listen to them, it will take your communication skills to another level. If you want to advance, you have to check your ego at the door. Remember, if the Lead Pastor is not willing to change and devote himself to personal development, then the church is not going to change or grow.

Creative Team:

This team's job is to create and design the elements of the services. Their responsibility is to enhance the overall experience for the audience. This team functions best with six to ten people.

The Creative Director takes the notes from the teaching team's meeting. The Creative Team then begins coming up with ideas for the services based on these themes. This process begins six weeks prior to the launch of a new teaching series.

Ideas from this team will include: Series branding, staging, special songs, videos, dramas, illustrations, etc.

The best way to utilize this group of creative-types is to be as visual as possible because that's how they are wired. An example would be using a white board to map out the four to five-week sermon series. All ideas and elements are listed below each sermon title as they are presented. After all ideas are given, we begin to narrow the options. Once the service is planned, everything is passed on to the Logistics Team.

Logistics Team:

This team consists of only a few people. They take all the information from the Creative Team, detailing and organizing it, listing all the responsibilities, so that specialized personnel can carry out their assigned duties.

Project Manager:

This role is to ensure that everyone is staying on task and meeting deadlines. It's the Project Manager's job to coordinate all the various aspects of the projects and the personnel required to fulfill what the creative team has designed. To see that each team member clearly understands their responsibilities, timelines are created with assigned deadlines, to ensure that quality work is done at every level.

Service Producer:

Being a service producer means being the central brain of any service or production. This person will play a pivotal role in helping make weekend services run to perfection. Producing a service consists of creating a service schedule, making sure all video and on-screen content is loaded and ready to go, ensuring that all needed volunteers are scheduled and that responsibilities are clear. They lead our service run-through prior to the beginning of our first service. It's a complete service from start to finish. It's mandatory for every person who has any part in the service to attend. The producer analyzes everything, including what is being said, what people are wearing, and ironing out smooth transitions. Once the service begins, the producer is connected to all production personnel via headset microphone and directs every necessary production cue. This is a very intense role that requires a lot of dedication and an eye for excellence.

Post-Service Process:

This is where the Creative Director and the Service Producer meet with those involved in the service (sound, lighting, video production, stagehands, worship team, drama team, anyone speaking from the platform) for five to ten minutes. The purpose is to review the service and make any needed adjustments. This is done immediately following the first service to review and make any changes needed to enhance the following services.

Stagehands:

All stagehands are required to dress completely in black. It keeps them from being too visible while working on stage. They work backstage with scenery, props, and special effects. They play a vital role in any service by knowing exactly where and when to move props, equipment, staging, etc.

Worship Team:

Music plays a large role in creating a production-driven service. In addition to leading our church in a time of worship each week, our musicians and vocalists participate in preparing music for special services (Christmas, Easter, etc.) and cover songs to illustrate the theme of a service.

Videographers:

Videographers capture the stories of "real people" in our church family doing "real things." It could be their story of transformation or being involved in an outreach event, holiday celebration, or a Bible study. Video also becomes a powerful tool in communicating upcoming events through announcements during service times.

Web Designer:

We may have had the world's worst website. At the time we weren't able to hire a web designer, so we decided that our best option was to outsource that job for optimal results. We knew our website had to reflect our new image. As soon as we had the funds, we hired a full-time graphic and web designer who began doing all design work from print pieces to web pages.

Social Networking Guru:

Since communication these days has gone "viral," we wanted to make sure we were connecting with our church family and the local community through the latest technologies. This person is responsible for expanding and overseeing the online presence and influence of the church, posting information regarding the upcoming events and activities, and responding to comments on all church social media sites.

Camera Operator:

Our camera operators are a big part of the various services and experiences of the church. In our preparation to move into a larger auditorium, we began using live camera feed to video projection screens before we really needed this feature. Having done so meant that we had experienced camera operators once we did make the move. Cameramen also serve an incredible purpose in capturing the services to be placed on our website so that they can be viewed by church members who are out of town, or anyone who wants to be a part of the ministry but is unable to physically attend.

Sound Engineer:

These volunteers work to create the best possible environment for worship and teaching. This includes, but is not limited to, creating an audio mix that sets the mood that the pastor and worship leader want to convey. They also support the audio needs of everyone involved in a service or production.

Lighting Engineer:

The lighting engineer performs the necessary functions to meet the lighting needs of a weekend service. Whether the look is simple and understated or dazzling and full of excitement, the lighting is absolutely integral to the service production. They will work with the service producer in creating the best look possible to represent every element of the service. The lighting engineer is also responsible for maintaining all rigging and equipment.

Prayer Team Coordinator:

The Prayer Ministry Coordinator trains our prayer team and oversees the function of this ministry. This includes organizing the team for ministry in weekend services, nights of prayer, and special events.

Prayer Team:

Members of the prayer team are hand-selected to serve by the pastoral staff and Ministry Coordinator. After completing the required training, they are then added to the rotation of those who serve in weekend services. Additionally, members of the prayer team receive prayer requests throughout the week and remain in continual prayer for every aspect of the church.

Guest Experience Coordinator:

This coordinator oversees and manages the recruitment, training, and scheduling for all ministry associated with guest services. This includes I'm New, ushers, all greeters, and security. This team lead also ensures that all volunteers are dressed appropriately, including wearing their guest services lanyard and t-shirt.

Parking Lot Team:

Also known as the "first impressions" team, this team is the initial contact that attendees receive as they pull onto our campus. Beyond a smiling face and warm welcome, this team also provides additional assistance to those with wheelchairs, children, bags, etc. They also help monitor traffic flow in the parking lot before and after each service. The moment people step out of their cars, this team creates anticipation in the hearts of people before they ever get through the front doors.

I'm New Team:

At the center of our atrium is a designated area called I'm New. The purpose is to provide our guests with a central, visible location where they can find assistance and information. The team that serves in this area of ministry is highly informed on the various ministries and activities in the church.

Greeters:

Greeters are an essential part of our weekend experience. From the parking lot to the doors and from the entrance to the auditorium, our campus is covered with friendly people who make everyone who attends feel welcome.

Head Ushers:

The head usher schedules and oversees the various teams of ushers who serve over the course of our weekend services and any special event.

Ushers:

Our ushers stand ready to serve the needs of the congregation while in the auditorium. In addition to identifying the best seats available, our ushers assist with flow of operations during our prayer time as well as distributing communion and literature, as needed.

Security Teams:

Security team members help provide a safe, secure environment while attendees are on the grounds of our church. Their presence can be found both inside and outside of our facility ensuring the safety and surveillance of all people and property.

These are some examples of the detailed job descriptions that we put in place for our weekend services. We created descriptions like these for every area of ministry in the church.

Every job had a job description and a team leader. Everyone's responsibilities were very well defined. Each person was expected to carry out their assignment just as it had been spelled out. We did not want to leave any room for them to fall back into old routines, or what seemed the easiest, or what we had always done.

It's the craziest thing: Whenever you are leading a group of people to accomplish a task, everyone's an expert! Everyone has an opinion and is convinced their way is the best way. Sometimes I wonder if anyone ever just follows directions. We had a church full of people who had been in the church for twenty years and longer. The mentality had always been, "If I don't like a certain rule I'll just ignore it and do what I want to do." There was an unbelievable sense of entitlement.

This is extremely common in many well-established churches. Many people actually believed that they were above the rules because they had been there longer than the pastor. High demands, expectations, and accountability were a very new concept for us.

A couple of ladies on our staff, who had a gift for administration, did an amazing job of organizing, detailing and enforcing all expectations for our team leads and holding them accountable to carry out the plan.

A Culture Of Critique

One more vital component for the success of cultural change is developing a culture of critique among staff and volunteers. In the Christian community we tend to shy away from critical comments because we believe our spiritual duty is to be positive and encouraging with those with whom we are working. That is definitely an important part, but it must be coupled with positive critique – constantly challenging the "why" of everything we do. We must create a culture of critique among our teams if we have any hope of successful improvement.

> *We must create a culture of critique among our teams if we have any hope of successful improvement.*

If someone has constructive criticism, it means they want to give you feedback from a different perspective. It comes from a fresh set of eyes that see something we may have been entirely blinded to. In all of our meetings we encourage constructive criticism that will help us to improve and rise to a higher level.

Taking criticism can be a difficult thing. When someone's telling you how to do things better, it can be hard to deal with. After all, nobody likes to be told they're wrong. In the church world we can be very protective over our ministry turf. The last thing we want is someone challenging what we have poured our life into.

Creating a culture of critique means learning to listen and then being willing to move forward making the necessary improvements. Engaging in these conversations will help to enhance your performance, service, or events. Sometimes it will make for uncomfortable listening, but it can make your ministries stronger as a result.

Constructive criticism can guide you away from bad practices and toward good ones. Try to be objective and look at your specific ministry as though it's not yours, but ours. This can be particularly difficult when your heart and soul are involved, but if you can take a step back you might see how to improve and avoid negative outcomes down the road.

The language you use in response to criticism is vitally important. Try to avoid getting into an argument. Instead, turn the exchange into a discussion about how to resolve problem areas.

Remember these three things:

1. Show that you can listen to feedback, respond in the correct way, and make the needed changes. That speaks volumes to your coworkers. It makes you extremely valuable and a pleasure to work with.

2. Don't take it personally when someone doesn't like your work. Even if you feel you're being criticized unfairly, don't retaliate with an extreme knee-jerk reaction. Their thoughts and words are realistically pushing you to the next level which, after all, is everyone's goal.

3. Don't get offended. On occasion, you may feel like the criticism has become personal, and you may be right. There is just no way around it. We are all flesh and blood, and at times, even in ministry, our humanity gets the best of us. What we often say is, "Just put your big-boy pants on." In other words, don't allow yourself to be offended. We are a team, but every once in a while, unfortunately, our "flesh" will show itself when pushed out of our comfort zone. What everyone sitting around the table must remind themselves is that this critique is pushing them to a higher level of performance. This may be one of the hardest principals to learn, but it is also one of the most valuable.

Head-On Collision With The Head Greeter

One of the first big conflicts we had was when we were launching a new sermon series. Four weeks out, we wanted all of our greeters to wear t-shirts advertising the series. We purchased all the shirts and passed them out with great enthusiasm. The next weekend we had greeters showing up in their coat and ties and not the required t-shirt. Their response was, "I just don't feel comfortable wearing a t-shirt to church on Sunday morning." Some had defiance in their voice when they stated, "I'm not wearing it!" Now I'm talking about one man in particular who had been standing at those doors for thirty years greeting people his way. He was self-appointed as head usher and it was clear he didn't like the new way. What made matters worse, we had put a woman as his team lead and he was not going to take instructions from her. Well, our team leads had been instructed that everyone follows the rules. If we are a team, we function as a team.

One of the team leadership principles we were instilling into our volunteers was the value of teamwork. This is the definition we worked off of: "Teamwork is the ability to work together toward a common vision – the ability to direct individual accomplishments toward organizational objectives. It is the fuel that allows common people to attain uncommon results."

Again, building a team and implementing rules means nothing unless there is a clear purpose to the end result. For us, it was achieving excellence at every level.

The trap we fall into is when times get tough or in small beginnings we are tempted to cut corners. Never cut corners but always think "EXCELLENCE!" Excellence is not a goal that we will achieve someday. Excellence is a way of life. It's the care we take in our physical appearance, how we keep our house or how we take care of our vehicles. It's who we are. It comes to light in everything we do.

This was the principle we were conveying across the board with everyone. We were no longer going to continue doing the church thing at a common or average level, but we would pursue excellence at all costs. That means not doing the same old thing the same old way.

Let me share something with you that I came across the other day.

Excellence can be obtained if you:

...care more than others think is wise.

...risk more than others think is safe.

...dream more than others think is practical.

...expect more than others think is possible.

(*Posted by K. Sriram at tompeters.com.)

We so admire this quality of excellence in others and find ourselves wishing we could live at that level. I've thought often, "How long does it take for us to achieve excellence?" The answer is simple: It only takes a minute! We achieve excellence by promising ourselves right now that we will never again knowingly do anything that's not excellent. I'm not trying to be trite, it's just a fact.

Put in motion today a plan of excellence and don't back down or compromise...ever! Living at a level of excellence starts now. Choose how you're going to live.

Have you ever driven through the poorest part of your city and noticed all the surroundings? Dirt yards, broken-down cars, and car parts scattered everywhere. Paint chipping off the walls from not being repainted for years, weeds growing everywhere, things falling apart, and no attempt to fix anything. The whole neighborhood looks the same. Why? It's a defeated or poverty mentality. They probably think there is no use in even trying. But so many improvements could be done costing nothing except time and hard work – yet no effort is made. The principal of excellence has nothing to do with being rich or poor. It's a lifestyle decision and it will advance you at any level. The body of Christ needs to quit operating at a poverty level mindset. However little you might have, consider it a blessing. And what you do have, handle it with great respect and high value. What you value, others will value and improvements will begin.

> *The principal of excellence has nothing to do with being rich or poor. It's a lifestyle decision and it will advance you at any level.*

Now back to this greeter. As you can imagine, things didn't go well when he was told that he could not stand at the door and greet that morning because he refused to wear the mandatory t-shirt. Watching this scene unfold reminded me of the children's story I used to read so often to my kids entitled, "Alexander and the Terrible, Horrible, No Good, Very Bad Day." That's exactly what that day became, and I never saw him again after he walked out the door. These kinds of encounters are sad and unfortunate but inevitable. It's the very thing that helps us establish authority, team building and a new culture. Excellence!

We had our entire church focused on Sunday morning services and Student Ministries, and these two worked hand-in-hand with one another.

We had created such a large volunteer base that I was afraid we wouldn't have anyone actually sitting in the auditorium. We also started requiring all of our staff and volunteers to come to a complete run-through on Saturday afternoon. I was having a hard time believing this was really necessary, but larger churches did it, so we were going to do it. If you were making an announcement, then you came out on stage and said it just like you were standing before a live audience. Stagehands were there moving the podium and any other needed props on and off stage at the appropriate times. Every video was played. The worship team went through their whole worship set. No one was free to walk up on stage and shoot from the hip, saying whatever they wanted to say. Everything was scripted and practiced on stage. This was extremely awkward for everyone at first. It's painfully difficult walking out on a stage with a few people sitting in the auditorium critiquing everything you're saying and doing. If something didn't go right, we would stop and do it again.

Our camera crew was there taking notes and working on camera angles. We had never filmed any of our services before, but larger churches did it, so we were going to do it as well. Are you starting to get the idea? We really implemented everything a church of a thousand would, without excuses. We were working on a shoestring budget and the church didn't own any cameras. Our video team borrowed home video cameras from different individuals in the church and mounted them on cheap tripods at three different locations in the auditorium. Our camera crew was very serious about their job. They wore Radio Shack headphones and the video director was sitting at a switcher we had bought for a hundred and fifty dollars that enabled them to switch from camera one to camera two to camera three.

The funny thing about this camera crew was that for a year and a half they worked so diligently on all the different camera shots and angles, yet nothing was being recorded or broadcast – not on the auditorium screens or on our website. They were totally motivated by the vision that one day we would be in a new facility with state-of-the-art equipment and we were preparing for that day. We were all being driven by the thought, "One Day!"

> *The truth is that focusing on the future is what sets leaders and churches apart.*

The truth is that focusing on the future is what sets leaders and churches apart. The capacity to imagine and articulate exciting future possibilities is the defining mark of a real leader. They ask, "What's new? What's next?" They think beyond what's directly in front of them. As you lead people through a transition, keep in mind that the people following you want to know where you plan to take them. They want you to share that glimpse of the future. You have to clearly paint the portrait so they can actually see the beauty of tomorrow.

Serving became a cornerstone of our church. Within weeks I actually began to sense spiritual health being restored into our people. Serving: What an amazing concept! It shouldn't really surprise any of us. It's exactly the principle Jesus taught when showing us how to win the world. Going back to what I addressed earlier about self-centered Christianity, are we a church centered on continued learning year after year for the sake of learning, or are we learning how to leave the classroom to impact the world around us?

I was sitting at my son, Jonathan's, graduation with all of our family and friends as we watched him walk across the stage to receive his Doctor of Pharmacy diploma. He had just finished his sixth year at the University of New Mexico. What a great accomplishment! The first day at his new job he was only twenty-three years old. He was walking in that day as the lead pharmacist and it was rather nerve-racking, to say the least. Worried and anxious? Absolutely! Feeling like he wasn't completely prepared to deal with every issue? No question about it! After six long years of sitting in a classroom, he was now thrown into the field, doing what he was trained to do – positively effecting hundreds of lives every day through medical advice and prescription medications. Being plunged into the field of medicine, within a very short amount of time, his knowledge of pharmacy greatly increased beyond the classroom setting. When we mix our training with actual experience we become a master of the trade. Being educated without hands-on experience is nothing but useless theory.

The church would do well to learn from this university model. Train them and send them to the field. Oh, wait a minute! That is also the Biblical model that Jesus taught. In Mark 16:15, He said to them, "Go into all the world and preach the gospel to all creation." The concept is train, send, win!

So many churches get caught up in making their entire existence about teaching instead of teaching with the purpose and design to mobilize our people into the field. That last step is one that has never been properly employed in many churches.

The small group concept that has been so popular in the last fifteen years is now beginning to shift. Small groups have been highly effective, but for many they have run their course. You can see this shift happening all across our nation in our local churches. A new wave is moving and growing to get people out of their home groups and turn them into community service groups. I believe this new cultural swing is going to produce the greatest days the church has ever seen in our nation. Young pastors are rising up and leading this new direction. I don't think there has ever been a generation as cause-oriented. They are highly motivated by community projects and worldwide service opportunities. Instead of small groups, where Christians meet with Christians every week, they are shifting to Christians serving the poor, widows, hurting, and lost. This mentality is going to once again move the church outside of its walls and into the community where it needs to be. It's amazing to think how just one individual church that picks up this simple concept can have the ability to impact hundreds of lives surrounding them every day.

Spiritual education is overrated. Now don't go ballistic on me! If you've been in church very long, you know exactly what I mean. There is a time to get out of the classroom and to start putting the principles of Christ into practice. When we shifted our church model from sitting and receiving to coming and serving, spiritual maturity began to explode.

No matter what church you are a part of, it will not become a growing, thriving church until this shift has been achieved. When the church creates a culture of servanthood mixed with excellence, watch out because big things are about to happen!

Chapter 10

The Enormous Power of Beholding the Vision

Vision always starts with foresight. It is invisible. It only exists in thought. It's a hope. It is a dream that is not a physical reality. Vision is exciting, motivating, and keeps us hopeful for tomorrow. But there is nothing like the tangible fulfillment of that which was once just a thought – when one day what you have dreamed of begins to play out before your very eyes. As I reflect back on everything we did, I'm convinced we make church growth too difficult. It's all about simplicity. Let me recap and remind you of this simple process:

> First, we started with a crystal clear vision.
> Second, we narrowed our focus through elimination.
> Third, we moved to what I call the observation stage.

Observation Stage

I want to take a moment and talk about how crucial this step is for success.

While moving into this stage we created three very intentional steps so that people could observe the vision being birthed before their very eyes.

I came across one of Ed Young's sermon series entitled, "The Table." This series reinforced the idea that as followers of Christ we become hosts and hostesses for the Kingdom of God. At the table, there is always room for one more. The three messages were, "Bring others to the table," "Pushing away from the table to serve others," and "Accepting Christ's invitation to the table."

He talked about how, in his opinion, the church should be divided up into thirds. In a healthy church one-third of the congregation would be mature Christians, one-third would be baby Christians, and one-third would be hell-bounders. When I looked at this, it just made sense to me. It was a constant cycle of Christians bringing in the lost, exposing them to the message of Christ, and then training them to reproduce themselves. This is the ministry machine that Christ put into motion.

I took this concept and did a five-week teaching series with a huge table on the stage. During the message, I had people prepared to join me on stage who had experienced life-change through Christ since attending our church. These were amazing stories of how messed up their lives were, but after accepting an invitation to church, they gave their lives to Christ and everything changed. Almost all of these testimonies were coming out of our college ministry.

Their testimonies were so powerful and moving that many people in the audience wept when hearing how Christ and His church had changed them. When those five weeks were over I knew we were onto something. Every person in our church vividly realized that together we were changing lives. A buzz began to spread around the city as people were excitedly talking about the great things happening in our church.

When I completed this series, realizing the tremendous impact these life-changing stories were having on our people, I knew it could not stop. The next three things I did turned the cultural tide faster than I could have ever imagined.

1. Tell The Story

From that moment, every staff member and volunteer leader was required to help identify life-change stories that could be shared. For the next year and a half I had a small table on stage and somewhere in my message I would invite someone to sit down at the table with me and they would share their story of life-change. During the week I personally sat down with these people, working through their stories so they would be able to convey it with the highest impact. Many times I visited with the ones who were too shy or just unable to present very well, so I would have them sit with me and I would tell their story for them.

I cannot emphasize this enough: This one simple thing transformed us and was the catalyst in moving our entire congregation to a missional mindset. There is nothing more powerful than being a part of something bigger than ourselves. A healthy pride began to grow among our congregation. People began to believe that if they invited someone to church, *they* would have an encounter with God as well. Something radical had changed in the atmosphere.

2. Communicate the story

This second thing that had tremendous impact in moving us quickly down the road toward reaching our vision was great communication. As I mentioned earlier, I communicated our vision at small groups in homes for sixteen straight nights. It was vision-casting and fielding questions about our new direction. I had conveyed it time and again from the platform, and yet I could tell that many had not fully bought in or understood.

So, several months later I reinforced the communication of our vision on a Sunday night by calling all of our church leadership team and staff together. I wanted everyone to fully understand and champion the cause. As they all gathered, everyone was being inquisitive about why they were invited to this meeting. Many were making jokes, asking each other what crazy changes were going to be made next, because change became the name of the game. Walking into that room full of people was the best feeling in the world. Never had I been around such positive, eager, enthusiastic people. The personality of our church had completely changed. I could actually feel the unity and excitement in the room. That old feeling of contention – people fighting and defending their own personal agendas or resisting change – was gone. This is a sad thing to say, but after all these years of being in the ministry, I now understood the New Testament phrase, "Brothers and Sisters." I felt like I was among family.

That night I pulled up a stool and asked them to help me move our vision down the road a little faster. "I need every person in our church to be extremely clear in our direction and why we have made all of these changes."

The purpose of this meeting was to give our people time to process and digest why we must continue to change. It was creating a church-wide attitude of embracing rather than resisting. What makes this even more challenging in a well-established church versus a church plant is the deprogramming process. Before people embrace change, they have to unlearn old ways and methods. People instinctually will hear change as what you are taking away from them. The goal in vision casting is to always convey what they will gain through the change. As leaders, leading the change is a balancing act in being sensitive yet steadfast at the same time.

> *The goal in vision casting is to always convey what they will gain through the change.*

After crystal clear vision-casting and open discussion we come to the third step.

3. Celebrate the story

We created what we call "Celebration Services" that we held quarterly. These are specially designed weekend services filled with many creative elements highlighting life-change. We try to blow this one out of the creative box.

In these services I will only speak for about fifteen minutes and then end my message with water baptisms. Only a year before, on a rare occasion, we would baptize four or five people at a time. The sad thing was that it was never very exciting. We re-thought how we would present baptisms. This should truly be the greatest celebration of any kind. After all, this is the sole reason of our existence – leading people to Christ. Baptism is the celebration of people being added into Heaven, and there is no greater cause.

For the service finale our worship team comes back out on stage. Our Worship Pastor has everyone stand and leads them in a powerful, uplifting song. That Sunday morning as the church raised the roof in their worship, I baptized seventy-five people, and most of them were teens and college students. As each one would come up out of the water, the place exploded in applause and loud cheers. There wasn't a dry eye in the room.

Something had happened and something was different as the vision was unfolding before our very eyes. The vision that we had declared by faith – to win a young generation – was no longer simply a hope, but it had become a reality. We were a church of all ages reaching a young generation!

The amount of people now accepting Christ during just one weekend was more than the last ten years all put together. Everything we did was with simplicity, woven with creativity, and presented at the highest level of excellence possible.

Momentum, Make The Most Of It

We were now filling our building for two Sunday morning services, and the discussion came up in a staff meeting about going to three services. That created tremendous anxiety for me. The reason I was so anxious was because of the flashbacks I had, recalling the day we made the decision to go to two services. At that time, we had a partially full service and a very poorly attended service. Walking out on stage to preach or to lead worship for a few scattered people in the auditorium was like standing before the living dead. After we had created a poorly attended, dead service, we were stuck with it for a long time. People would try that service and never return. I dreaded that service, and our worship team found it painfully difficult.

That memory caused me to think long and hard about starting another service and repeating the same mistake. But I also knew that when you have momentum you cannot jeopardize it by a fear of the past.

> *But I also knew that when you have momentum you cannot jeopardize it by a fear of the past.*

So, after laboring for many hours over the decision to start a third service, we came up with a plan. When it comes to multiple services this is one of the most important things to remember: Don't let people just show up to whatever service they choose and hope it all works out. Just hoping that a good crowd will attend the new service is a risk you do not want to take. The leadership team must dictate the result they want to ensure. We carefully calculated how many people we would need in each service to make it look full enough to create life and energy.

After many hours of planning, we began advertising the launch of our third service five weeks in advance. All ushers and greeters wore T-shirts all five weeks with a big "3" encompassed by a circle as advertisement. In our foyer we had a table set up with three large glass containers and each one was filled with wristbands. Each container represented a service time. The first container was filled with yellow wristbands, the second with red, and the third with purple. When they chose a wristband we asked them not to take it off for the next five weeks and to use it as a conversation starter to invite someone to church. When I announced the new service times I approached it with the idea of planting a new service – much like planting a new church. I asked for one hundred and fifty people to make a six-month commitment to help us grow this new service. Within the next few weeks, after everyone had taken a wristband, we knew how many people were going to be in each service.

If the services were not balanced as we had planned, we would ask people to shift services. For example, "We need 40 of you to volunteer to exchange your red wristband for a purple one." When we started the third service all three were very balanced and we lost no momentum. If you don't prepare well then you will spend all your time repairing what you did not prepare for. There is a small difference between the two words, "Prepare" and "Repair", yet it's the difference between success and failure. Preparation is looking into the future with a plan. You can choose to spend your time in the agony of repairing or the joy of preparing for an amazing future.

John F. Kennedy said it like this, "The time to repair the roof is when the sun is shining."

Don't just let things happen – make things happen successfully.

I love the statement Johnny Carson once said, "Talent alone won't make you a success. Neither will being in the right place at the right time, unless you are ready. The most important question is: 'Are you ready?'"

With so many teens and college students coming to the church, we found that their parents soon followed and our crowds were increasing. In our tiny building we went from three services to four services and continued to grow until we added a fifth service. We were bursting at the seams in every area. Excitement was at an all-time high simply because we had prepared well.

Chapter 11

Just Doodling on a Piece of Paper

When we launched this lofty vision of reaching a young generation, we were very unsure how it would be accomplished. We were committed to its success even though we didn't know what success would look like. What I've learned is that vision is simply an undeniable passion to achieve a dream – even if you don't know how to get there or what the end result will be. When you have clearly decided on a direction, through much time and prayer, just state your dream and go!!

> *When you have clearly decided on a direction, through much time and prayer, just state your dream and go!!*

Here is how this amazing story unfolds...

Our son Dustin, while still in college, was sitting in a leadership class on a Sunday morning in the church he was attending. His mind drifted off and he started daydreaming about what he would do upon graduating. He had a great desire to be a student pastor and his dream was to work with me in the church he loved and in which he grew up. As he was doodling on a piece of paper about potential names for a youth ministry, he wrote down 212 (this number in Fahrenheit is the boiling point of water). Whenever water rises to a temperature of two hundred and twelve degrees, it changes states. When a teapot is filled with water and placed on the stove, it will eventually reach two hundred and twelve degrees. The pot will begin whistling because the water has been transformed into steam. At this point of transformation, steam becomes an enormous power.

It was in the 1800's when man perfected the steam engine by harnessing this power. Steamboats and steam engine trains changed the world.

As Dustin continued to think about this process, he realized that most people live their lives in a lukewarm state, never reaching their full potential – their boiling point. You go to church and you love God, yet you're simply living an average Christian life like everybody else. But Dustin didn't want to be average in any way, shape, or form. He wanted to live life at 212 degrees – where everything changes. Christianity was designed to be lived at the boiling point - the place of transformative power.

If that kind of power is available, why would we ever choose anything less?

Sitting there that day, he had no idea of the power that moment held. What seemed to be just another ordinary day was anything but ordinary. This would be a day he would never forget. In a very quiet manner, God came down in that classroom and whispered in his ear, "2,000 in 2012." No lightning bolts, thunder, smoke, or fire, but a faint whisper. No one in the room that day heard anything. No one was aware that God Himself had just spoken to a young freshman in college who had nothing but a desire and a dream. He immediately wrote down the phrase, "2,000 in 2012." What does that mean?

Staring at his paper, he thought, "One day I will be a youth pastor over a student ministry called 212. And by the year 2012 we will be ministering to 2,000 students." That thought came out of nowhere.

He knew that this was not simply a random thought but that he had just heard from God. It seemed ridiculous! Two hundred students in 2012 would be a great accomplishment. Two thousand students seemed absolutely impossible.

It's at these moments when we all have to decide: Was this my own foolish thinking or is this what God is calling me to? We can think, "Who am I? I'm a nobody, without experience or obvious talents. What makes me think that I'm special enough to do what no one else is doing?" Or we can know without a doubt that we have heard from God and never let go of his Word. God has always created something out of nothing and although we may feel like a nothing, in the hands of God, we are something.

The temptation is always to second-guess ourselves and to believe that great exploits are for others – that our thoughts are nothing but wishful thinking on our part.

> *The temptation is always to second-guess ourselves and to believe that great exploits are for others*

I received a phone call from Dustin that evening and as always, I was thrilled to hear from him. I could always sense when he had something exciting to tell me.

He would start off by saying, "Dad, dad, you won't believe this!" That day, he went on, "Today at church I came up with the name of my future youth ministry. It's going to be 212, and in the year 2012 I'm going to have 2,000 students."

There must have been a long pause on my end of the phone because after a moment he said, "Dad, are you there? Did you hear what I said?" Oh yes…I had heard him. "Wow! That's great. I know you will do it!" That's what encouraging dads do. We lie!

I loved his enthusiasm, but it was a little over the top. My thought was that in a couple of years he will mature and set realistic goals. What else would I expect? He's just a kid.

What's so incredible to think about is that I'm the one who had cast the vision of reaching a young generation, yet 2,000 students was beyond what I could imagine. The size of my dream was challenged that day by childlike faith.

Joseph in the Old Testament was just a kid when God revealed his future to him in a dream. God-given visions, whispers, and dreams are sometimes dangerous to share. It put Joseph in a heap of trouble and almost cost him his life.

Solomon gave wise council when he said, "There is a time for everything, and a season for every activity under heaven." He continued, "...a time to be silent and a time to speak."

There is no shortage of dream-stealers in the world. It's hard to admit, but when we are displeased with our own lives, it's extremely difficult to watch others succeed. When we live mediocre and mundane lives, it's hard to see a family member or friend soar far beyond us. It's been said, "It's easier to weep with those who weep than to rejoice with those who rejoice."

I always find it amusing, watching a Miss America Pageant, when the winner is announced. All the other girls come out on stage with big smiles. They hug and kiss and congratulate the winner, telling her how beautiful she is and how happy they are for her. They aren't happy! They would like to kick her. As she starts her long acceptance walk, waving at all the people, they are all hoping she trips and falls off the stage. Inside they're hoping her crown falls off and shatters into a million pieces. They are all thinking, "I deserve it more than she does. It's not fair!"

Deep down we don't like other people showing us up. Consciously or subconsciously people will try to convince you to give up on your dream – telling you it's foolish thinking. So we let go of our dream and fall into place with all the other "normal" people.

That's why you need to keep your dream tightly tucked away and close to your heart. There is a time to share it and a time to hold it. And that's the advice I gave Dustin. When you share dreams like that, it can make you look prideful and arrogant when realistically it's your confidence in God and His purpose for your life.

Upon Dustin's graduation he was hired as the church's new Student Ministries Pastor. The Sunday morning that I announced him as our new Student Pastor he was absolutely beaming with excitement. Unfortunately, this day was not without incident. A prominent couple in our church, who had attended for many years, got up and walked out in the middle of the announcement. As they walked down the aisle they shook their heads in disapproval. They were making a strong statement of opposition. He took issue with me hiring my son, but the real issue was that he wanted me to hire a full-time staff member to lead our senior adults group. He believed a volunteer could run the youth ministry. After that morning service I was standing at the door visiting with people for an unusually long time and enjoying visiting with different ones as they were leaving. This older couple who had walked out had returned and I saw them walking across the foyer towards me. He reached out and handed me a letter. The only thing he said was, "We will not be back!"

I opened up the envelope and inside was the resignation from his position as a ministry leader. He also notified me that a copy had already been given to all of our church board members. He was appalled that I had the audacity to hire a family member. This had been brewing for several weeks and he had already influenced a sizable group of people. Immediately, several older couples followed him to another church that had a stronger focus on senior adults.

Well that created a bumpy start, but by now we were used to the rugged terrain of public opinion. Dustin was following his own youth pastor, who had been in that position for ten years. He was a very gifted speaker and was moving to another city to plant a new church. He remains one of my dearest friends to this day. Dustin had big shoes to fill…and it was intimidating.

Following someone with that kind of tenure is difficult, so we decided to shut down the youth program for one month, giving Dustin the best shot for a smooth transition and a successful new beginning. Three years had now passed from his freshman year in college but he still had the crinkled piece of paper on which he had written the vision. The week following Dustin's appointment onto our staff we took the first step in fulfilling the dream by changing the name of our student ministry to 212. He found resistance immediately. Students who were attached to the former youth pastor were asking, "Why did he have to leave? We like the name we've had for the past eight years. Why do you have to come in here and change everything?" But what no one knew was that this was the beginning of an extraordinary journey that God had ordained.

Through the transition from one youth pastor to another the student attendance had now dropped to about thirty kids.

During the previous summer Dustin and several of his old high school friends took on the challenge I had given them to build a college and young adult group to a hundred people. Remarkably, they accomplished that task. This became our source of leadership for middle and high school ministries. In a very clear and precise manner we communicated to the parents in our church that we want to come alongside you and help empower you to raise Godly, talented kids who influence the nations. We told them that we were going to provide the best children's ministry, which would flow into an exceptional student ministry, which would then funnel into our young adults ministry. In all three stages we would help develop their talents and empower them to be leaders. When they entered into marriage and a career, they would be prepared to face the world and to succeed.

The new focus of our church was serving. These college-aged students rallied around Dustin's vision and volunteered to help wherever they could. College students with the gift of administration started organizing, those with the gift of leadership started leading, and those with the gift of serving started serving. For most of them this was the first time they had ever operated in their gifting, and many were completely unaware what their natural gift was. I sat back and watched in amazement the extraordinary talent and leadership that started rising up. This leadership team continued to grow in number. Every time I walked down one of the church hallways, they were meeting. They had meetings upon meetings upon meetings. They were constantly dreaming, planning, mapping, training, and this young crowd became the greatest leaders in our church.

We highlighted our students in our weekend services often through testimonies, music, drama, ballet, and video announcements. Three years later we had a middle school and high school ministry of about two hundred and a college and young adult service of about a hundred and twenty.

In fulfilling the vision of reaching a young generation, nothing had been easy.

Trying to get students to come to our church, when the outward appearance screamed old and boring, was challenging. There were all kinds of power struggles and egos among this young leadership group.

A group of five or six college students launched a vicious attack against Dustin and the vision. They would catch him as he was walking off the stage to inform him of all of his mistakes and challenged him on what he really meant by a certain statement. "You don't preach the Word. This church is unbiblical. The vision isn't properly aligned, and I could lead better than you." They were constantly criticizing, and it started to take a toll on Dustin. I watched the light of excitement fade. His driving energy to build the ministry was now stolen by fighting opposition and the enormous stress that leaves you exhausted. I watched him lose confidence while catering to certain demands, trying to make them happy.

One young lady, who grew up in our church, always seemed to be in the middle of every negative discussion. Well, she jumped on the bandwagon with the criticizers and called a meeting with Dustin. She started the meeting saying, "God has revealed something to me." She opened up her super-sized Bible and handed it to him. She made him read the story aloud about King David and his adulterous affair. When he finished it, she said, "God has revealed to me that you will fall morally and you will be completely out of the ministry by December." She got up and walked out the door.

Those kinds of meetings leave you stunned and speechless. These kinds of people will suck the life, energy, and time from those called to give life, and these kinds of actions and attacks never stop.

The reason I mention this is because I've gone to too many conferences and church growth meetings that talk about growth, change, expansion, and miracles, and it all sounds like their process was a tiptoe through the tulips.

I never want to paint the wrong picture. Ministry is war! The gates of Hell will open up and pour out its best to stop anybody who desires to advance the Kingdom.

However, after thirty years of ministry, I can also tell you that there's not a demon in Hell that can stop what God has placed in you. All the jabs, the criticisms, the hurtful words, and all the seeming dead ends are nothing but a rattling noise. Don't ever get knocked off track by the noise.

> *after thirty years of ministry, I can also tell you that there's not a demon in Hell that can stop what God has placed in you.*

The first few years the student ministry attendance was like a roller-coaster, up and down with no consistency. Dustin had worked hard trying to get on the high school campuses around the city. Most of them were very reluctant to allow him on campus, but he had managed to start and lead three Bible clubs at different schools – however, none of them seemed to be overly successful. The school year ended for summer break and 212 leadership spent the summer planning to make a big impact on school campuses the following year.

When the new school year started they approached the school's administration to find that a new policy had been established and youth pastors were no longer allowed on campus. There seemed to be a strong sense of animosity against the church. What they had worked on and put so much time into during the summer months was now a shattered dream. They were completely barred from every school.

One month later Dustin received a call from one of the high school counselors. She said his name had been recommended to her and she needed his help. Their high school was in a very low-income area of town and the school district was threatening to shut down the school because one third of the senior class was failing. She explained that most of these kids were from poor and broken homes with little parental support. If they didn't turn this around fast, they were in trouble. She said, "Dustin, we need after-school mentors to help get these kids to a passing grade."

Immediately, our college and young adult ministry organized a large group of people who were willing to give their time. It was an amazing connection with the public school system and they were thrilled by the results. Dustin strongly felt that he somehow needed to pursue the schools again. He called every high school and set up an appointment with every principal. At the very first meeting, Dustin explained how he wanted to be a positive influence in students' lives and that he just wanted to know how he could assist in making their job easier. The other thing he asked was could they have a Bible club on their campus? One principal seemed very nervous as Dustin talked about Bible clubs. He stood up abruptly and said, "I don't want to know anything else about these Bible clubs because I think it's against school policy. But, I want you to talk to someone else." The principal left the room and returned with one of the school counselors. "The two of you need to discuss this without me being present." And with that, the principal walked out of the room. Dustin thought, "How odd!" As he proceeded telling the counselor that he wanted to have a spiritual impact upon the students' lives, the councilor interrupted him and said, "I'm also a Christian." Dustin said, "What I need is permission to the start a Bible club on campus." Immediately, tears started flowing down the counselor's face as he said, "I've been praying for this moment for a long time. Our schools are in desperate need of God."

Dustin said it felt like an underground church was being planted as they both whispered so no one else could hear the details of their plans. At the end of the meeting the counselor reaffirmed the policy that he would not be allowed on campus but that he would help Dustin start a Bible club that would be completely run by students. Dustin could feel that God was up to something... and something big.

The public schools are one of the darkest places in our nation, the place God is needed the most and the place they have completely shut Him out.

One of our college-aged students joined up with Dustin to take the lead on opening as many Bible clubs as possible. Soon after, high school after high school opened up their doors and students began to be trained to treat these clubs like church plants within the schools. Today, hundreds of students meet each week. Dustin says all the time that the greatest thing the school did was not allow youth pastors on the campus because it has empowered students to rise up and lead. And lead they did – with great zeal! These young leaders of today will be the ones who change our world!

Well, it was only a few years ago, having only about thirty teenagers, that we blurted out this vision with a passion to reach a young generation. Just as we had narrowed our church's vision down to Sunday services, at that same time we were just as focused with student ministries, and it was definitely paying off. More and more kids were coming and absolutely packing out our church auditorium. They were showing up every day as soon as school was over for practices, meetings, service prep, or just hanging out, while many others were there because they had major responsibilities in weekend services for which they were preparing. It became so chaotic with students everywhere in our small building that at times I could hardly hear myself think as I prepared for the Sunday message. That is one thing about teenagers: They are incredibly loud! But I would sit in my office with a smile on my face. Their loudness was music to my ears. The crowds of teens continued to grow to the point that I finally gave up my office to provide them with a workspace and green room for their youth services. It continued to grow until we were forced to divide middle school from high school. We were now jamming our auditorium with high school students on Tuesday nights, middle school on Wednesday nights, and our college and young adult service on Thursday nights.

Today, 212 has expanded to the point of having four different satellite campuses and five network campuses, which are student ministries they have revitalized in smaller churches.

I want to tell you about one of these satellite churches. The church was a hundred years old with about forty people in total attendance. A young pastor had gone there hoping to do a great work but was met with resistance from people who had literally been in the church for over fifty years and whose parents had grown up in that church as well. You can imagine the near impossible task that it would be to change anything at all. When we met him, he was very discouraged and was talking to us about resigning. They had nothing for the younger generation. Their city is only about twenty thousand in population. It's also the home of Eastern New Mexico University – with about 6000 students – and he desperately wanted to reach the younger crowd. When we looked at his situation, we couldn't help but think, "And we thought we had it bad!" I remember someone telling me once, "Someone always has an uglier dog." Our situation had been ugly, but his was even uglier. He had watched our transformation and he would give anything to do the same in his community. It was hard to give him advice because I'm not sure I had ever seen a more difficult case. His congregation was concreted into old tradition and it wasn't changing. He shared stories of what he had gone through and it was absolutely unimaginable. Then, out of nowhere, this young pastor said to Dustin, "Why don't we advertise a college service at our church? We will show your sermons on video."

Dustin said, "I've never heard of doing a youth or college service like that, but let's try it." Our young leadership team packed up in the church van and traveled almost two hundred miles. They spent two days on the college campus in this small town passing out invitations to their launch service along with free food and drinks.

We assembled a worship team that committed to making this three-hour drive every Tuesday. Within six months they were averaging one hundred college students every Tuesday night in this small church. The pastor started recruiting many of these students to take on responsibilities for weekend services.

Several months later this young pastor asked Dustin to launch a 212 mid and high school service mimicking everything they had done with the plant of the college service. Within a few months they were also avenging between 80-100 teenagers.

The church that was unmovable and hadn't grown in years has recently gone to their third Sunday morning service with several hundred people attending. Today, this young pastor loves life and ministry again. I love that! It can happen to anyone and in any situation – larger churches partnering with smaller churches to accelerate their ability to reach the lost. This has happened over and over with our satellite campuses and network churches finding new life through reaching the young generation in their communities. This is part of the vision that we could have never imagined – larger churches empowering smaller churches.

> Vision always outgrows the initial dream.

Vision always outgrows the initial dream. From the day we declared, "We are going to be a church of all ages reaching a young generation," to where we are now, shows the power of focused vision.

Our youngest son Brandon recently graduated from the same university which Dustin had attended. We brought him on staff as our full-time college and young adult pastor. He's one of the finest people you will ever meet. He's everything good out of Kay and me. When we were looking for the best person to hire as a full-time college and young adult pastor, I didn't have to look very far. Within a year and a half, under his leadership, this group has doubled in size. During his four years in college he watched the vision unfold and couldn't wait to be a part of it. From day one of his hire there was a driving passion because, after all, it's his home, his church, and the people he loves. His story alone will be amazing to watch.

Today, we are ministering each week to an average of 550 students in the public schools, 950 students that meet at our main location and another 500 students gather at our satellite campuses.

This all happened in 2012 and that's extremely significant. Dustin still has that very worn, crinkled piece of paper that he doodled on years before – 2,000 in 2012.

Several years ago I heard a young college kid verbalize a foolish dream, and yet I watched it unfold into reality. A dream is unstoppable when mixed with a pin-pointed focus and tenacity!

Chapter 12

Take a Bite Out of the Apple

I was on my way to Mombasa, Kenya and had a long layover in the Atlanta Airport. While waiting, I walked into a bookstore looking for something to occupy my time on the eternal flight I was about to embark upon. I was drawn to the leadership and business section where I stood amazed at how many books have been written about the Apple success story. All the titles were very intriguing, which made for a difficult decision. I finally ended up purchasing a Carmine Gallo book called, "The Apple Experience." Later that evening as I got settled in on the plane, and cruising above the Atlantic Ocean, I pulled out this book. In it Gallo shares Apple's secrets to building insanely great customer loyalty.

"The Apple Experience" is about Steve Jobs and the principles that can transform any organization.

The Apple Store is the most profitable retailer in America, generating an average of $5,600 per square foot and attracting more than 20,000 visitors a week. I was so intrigued as I read through each principle because they centered on people first and business second.

These are simple and practical leadership concepts that can also be applied when thinking about improving the entire workings of the greatest organization on earth, the local church. What's remarkable about Apple's core beliefs is how much they center around Biblical principles, although I'm sure that was not their intent. These five simple principles took them to another level, and they can also greatly influence the operations of the local church.

1. Enrich Lives

When Steve Jobs first started the Apple Store he did not ask the question, "How will we grow our market share by 20 percent?" Instead he asked, "How do we enrich people's lives?"

Just as Apple is in the people business, so is the church. Many times the church makes the same mistakes as the business world. We are asking the wrong question. Instead of asking, "How do we grow by 20 percent in attendance and finances?" we should ask the real question, "How do we enrich people's lives?"

The Apple Store is so vested in this vision that the first two words on a wallet-sized credit card that the employees are encouraged to carry is, "enrich lives." When you enrich lives, magical things start to happen. For example, enriching lives convinced Apple to have a non-commissioned sales floor where employees feel comfortable spending as much time with a customer as the customer desires. Enriching lives led Apple to build play areas (family rooms) where kids could see, touch, and play on computers. Enriching lives led to the creation of a "Genius Bar" where trained experts are focused on building relationships as much as fixing problems.

What Apple discovered is that they need to slow down their employees and engage with people. Look at how they describe the Geniuses working at the bar.

"Geniuses have extensive knowledge of our products, and they work with you face to face to provide technical support and troubleshoot any problems. Want to meet with a Genius? Make a reservation ahead of time to guarantee your spot."

This idea inspired me to design our new facility with huge wide open spaces that include comfortable and spacious seating areas, a large, welcoming fireplace, a coffee shop that has a circular bar where people can sit and watch sports or the news, and an extensive area adjacent to the coffee shop furnished with tables and chairs for people to visit together or catch up on some work. The idea is to slow people down long enough to engage with one another. This is an environment created to enrich lives.

Also, instead of having a typical information desk, why not create a Genius Bar concept as well? The Genius Bar is equipped with a well-trained team who stand ready to answer questions, to pray with people, and to direct them to certain ministries that could enhance their lives.

They stand ready to work with people face to face, providing answers and support to advance their spiritual walk. Many people want to grow spiritually but have no idea how to get started, or their busy lives don't allow time for small groups or Bible studies. The Genius Bar concept is much like the fast-food concept. I don't have time to go in and sit down in a restaurant but I'm hungry, I'm in need of something, just make it fast. People who are too busy, undisciplined, or maybe even intimidated by getting involved in a small group or Bible study can stop by the Genius Bar and within five minutes a specialized genius can help resource them. A wide range of "Life Principal Cards" have already been predesigned for specific struggles people may be dealing with. A card dealing with their specific problem is handed to them with easy-to-follow, step-by-step principles to apply for thirty days. In no way is this to take the place of structured Bible classes but for some this is at least the start of getting God's word into their hearts and minds. When someone approaches the Genius Bar, no one feels rushed because their only purpose is enriching lives by giving them time and the right tools.

2. Hire for smiles.

The soul of the Apple Store is in its people. They are hired, trained, motivated, and taught to create magical and memorable moments for their customers. I love that! When I read that, I thought, "That's exactly the church's responsibility."

In the same way the soul of the church is its people. Volunteers are trained, motivated, and taught to create unforgettable moments for every guest who walks through our doors. Our church doesn't care how knowledgeable you are, how well you can teach, or how talented you are. The bottom line is the smile on your face. Christianity should never convey that we are sour and unpleasant people. This is the reason why we invest in and train our guest services team to operate at the highest level of hospitality. They are the ones who create an unforgettable atmosphere because we are not focused on programs and rigid rules, but we are truly focusing on and caring for people.

3. Celebrate diversity.

Mohawks, tattoos, and piercings are all acceptable among Apple Store employees. Apple hires people who reflect the diversity of their customers. Since they are more interested in how passionate you are, your hairstyle doesn't matter to them.

In today's world the name of the game, in reaching the lost, is "diversity." As I mentioned earlier, our goal as a church is to be made up of diverse thirds – the mature, the baby Christians, and the hell-bounders. That's a tremendously diverse group of people all coming together under one roof. An atheist, Christian, Republican, Democrat, the arrogant, the insecure, rich, poor, single, married, divorced, straight, gay, sick, and the healthy. That's the picture of a healthy church. The reason I'm so convinced of that is because it mirrors the crowds Jesus attracted and with whom He spent time. It is so strange to me how human nature hasn't changed much in two thousand years. The religious were confused and frustrated by the fact that He loved hanging out with a diverse group of people – who you might say were the good, the bad, and the ugly. These were people opposite of

Himself. Over time, the religious hated him for it and did their best to destroy His name, all because He believed in diversity.

At Copper Pointe Church, dreadlocks, tattoos, piercings, long hair, a shaved head, beards, and goatees are all acceptable on our platform. Our worship team and leadership will reflect the diversity of the people in our community – making a strong statement that this is not a cookie-cutter church where everyone looks like the stereotypical Sunday morning Christian. I've been there and done that, and no thanks. I don't want to do that again. Stereotypical churches many times create segregation and exclusiveness instead of being inclusive in which all might hear the greatest news in the world. Being inclusive doesn't mean we gloss over and accept sinful lifestyles, but we are fully expecting God to do in their life what He has done in ours.

> *Stereotypical churches many times create segregation and exclusiveness instead of being inclusive in which all might hear the greatest news in the world.*

4. Empower employees.

Apple has a non-commissioned sales floor for a reason. Employees are not pressured to "make a sale." Instead they are empowered to linger with a customer as long as it takes and do what they believe is the right thing to do.

Copper Pointe's "sales floor" is our atrium. We empower our people to be very intentional about their weekend schedule. Our church culture is that everyone arrives 15 minutes before service time and stays 15 minutes after the service solely to connect with people. Whether we are sitting at the coffee shop, seated on a comfortable couch, or in our lounge areas, we want our church family to be empowered to love, befriend, pray for, and minister to as many people as possible. We empower our people to linger and take as much time on our "sales floor" as it takes to bless and encourage someone.

5. Create multi-sensory experiences.

The brain loves multi-sensory experiences. In other words, people enjoy being able to see, touch, and play with products. Walk into an Apple Store and you'll see all the notebook computer screens perfectly positioned slightly beyond 90-degree angles. The position of the computer lets you see the screen (which is on and loaded with content) but forces you to touch the computer in order to adjust it. Every device in the store is working and connected to the Internet. Spend as much time as you'd like playing with the products, nobody will kick you out. Creatives who give one-on-one workshops do not touch the computer without asking for permission. They want you to do it. The sense of touch helps create an emotional connection with a product.

At the church level, we are intentional in creative thinking, providing an environment of multi-sensory experiences, and designing services that connect with the senses, creating a spiritual and emotional connection. Somehow we have to abolish an archaic belief that out-of-the-box churches, who find new methods of presenting the message of Christ, are sinful, shallow, and ineffective.

It's incredibly damaging when Christian leaders publicly bash other pastors and ministries because we disagree with their methods. We all see this embarrassing feud being played out on Facebook constantly. The pride that oozes out of so many pastors, leaders, and church attendees divides the Body of Christ instead of uniting us together and creating a force to reckon with.

So often we hear people slamming Rick Warren, Joel Osteen, Ed Young, and others for watering down the Gospel by calling them "feel good" preachers who provide little substance – when in reality they all are Biblically rock solid and are responsible for bringing tens of thousands into the Kingdom of God. Our problem is that we forget that it takes all kinds of methods and styles to reach all kinds of people. People learn differently.

Too often we look through such a narrow lens, convincing ourselves that our way of communicating the gospel is the Biblical way and the most effective way. It's fearful to think that so many are quick to criticize the different methods pastors use in presenting God's Word. Those who mock these pastors may actually be mocking God, who gifted them in a certain way to reach a certain group of people. That's a dangerous form of mockery.

The very thing that frustrated the religious in Jesus' day was the way he presented God's Word. For hundreds of years the Word of God was read word for word to the people. The Word of God was memorized word for word. The Rabi would stand in the front of the synagogue, open up the scrolls, and read it. But Jesus did something that no one had ever seen before. He took the Law and put it into story form (parables). He applied it to everyday life. It became relevant, and they understood it like never before. This is the reason why people would say, "We've never heard anyone speak like this!" It infuriated the religious leaders. "How dare he desecrate the Law." Why? Because it was different from what they had always done. It sounds like the debate and criticism we still hear today.

One of the most sad and immature things I've ever seen was when a very well-known pastor played a video clip of another well-known pastor of one of the largest churches in our country and maligned him in front of his congregation. It was a mockery of his entire ministry. Those kinds of actions divide the body of Christ to a greater degree than we could ever imagine. When a leader with national influence does something like this, it opens the floodgates for others to mimic those actions...and that's exactly what happened.

I can say with full confidence that the same pastor would have also mocked the teaching style of Jesus if He were teaching on earth today. Jesus' style was relational, creative, and simple enough that a child or an infidel would be able to understand it. And yet His message was life-changing. We have a world to reach, and it's going to take all of our unique differences to accomplish it. Let's applaud one another's differences, giftedness, and successes.

Three Primary Ways People Learn

For centuries, the traditional way churches have conveyed the Word of God was strictly in a lecture style. The problem with this approach is that only a portion of the people sitting in our congregations learn well by this style of communication. Here are three ways people learn:

1. Auditory Learners

These learners tend to lean more to the intellectual side. They learn best when information is methodically laid out. They love expository teaching, going verse-by-verse through scripture. That also means that if you don't learn well by hearing, you are out of luck. But you will find no shortage of people declaring that this style is an absolute – criticizing pastors who teach creatively and topically, as if that style is inferior. That is absolutely not true.

2. Visual Learners

These learn best by seeing what is taught. They are bored by long verbal presentations because their minds wander off so easily. They learn best when creative elements are intertwined into the presentation. They tend to gravitate to creative-style churches. That means, if you're pastoring this kind of church, you're going to have a whole lot of people with A.D.D. flooding into your doors. If you are a creative-style church, you might as well pass out Ritalin along with your church bulletin.

Also, in recent years, this younger generation has been so inundated with interactive technology that many of them will be drawn to this type of church environment. This is the reason why so many creative churches are exploding in growth today. They are speaking the language of the young and shattering the dreaded boring church concept. It's providing an environment of learning that they are accustomed to and comfortable with.

3. Interactive Learners

Interactive learners learn best through moving, touching and doing. They are much more oriented towards their feelings. They learn, not so much from lectures, but by actually doing something. The presentation must feel right or give them a "gut feeling." They gravitate to churches that are community service driven – a place where they can get their hands dirty. They thrive when they are ministering to the poor, homeless, elderly, abused and abandoned.

———•———

There are all types of people who have all kinds of needs. Have you ever looked at someone and thought, "that is one strange and weird person?" The reason why is because they are different from yourself. In the same way, we will look at churches that are different than what we are accustomed to and think they are weird and strange. We will be tempted to criticize them because we don't like or understand their methods. Instead of criticizing, celebrate their weirdness and thank God they are attracting the people you don't want to deal with or spend time with. There's always a silver lining.

We who are spiritual teachers and instructors need to be highly sensitive to our audience – those to whom we are trying to convey a message.

> *We who are spiritual teachers and instructors need to be highly sensitive to our audience – those to whom we are trying to convey a message.*

"Multisensory teaching" is becoming the new educational buzzword. Another phrase we're starting to hear is multisensory natural revelation. The thought is that God designed us to learn by what we see, hear, touch, smell, and taste. It's believed this is why Jesus so often taught spiritual truth with visual aids. Think about how often He did this by using water, wheat, branches, dirt, vines, a coin, an olive tree, and little children. Jesus was showing us how to communicate the most important information in the world in the most effective way. It was multisensory communication – hitting all three major ways people learn – verbal, visual and interactive. After decades of the church presenting the Gospel verbally, we now understand that this one-dimensional style is not the most effective way of communicating when trying to reach the masses. We desperately need all styles of churches for a wide range of people.

Chapter 13

The Nightmare That Wouldn't Stop

From the first day of pastoring our church I knew we would have to relocate if we had any plans for significant growth. Many years later the church board chose a couple of men to work with me to explore any possibilities of purchasing land. You might say we were just testing the waters. It quickly became very depressing. Finding any vacant property larger than eight to ten acres was almost impossible.

We half-heartedly looked for property for the next three years, realizing it would take an absolute miracle to buy enough land to relocate. That year I went on a missions trip for pastors to Kenya, Africa. We were riding in four-wheel-drive jeeps for six hours down dry riverbeds headed to a very remote tribe that was totally isolated from the modern world. While riding together, we were enjoying sharing stories of the wonderful things God was doing in our churches. One of the pastors sitting in the front seat started sharing an amazing story of how their church had just completed a new facility. The story he told was absolutely unbelievable! Their congregation had their eye on twenty acres of the most prime property in Ft. Worth, Texas, right off the interstate. It was priced millions of dollars beyond what they could afford. In faith, the church continued to pray that God would make a way. While they were waiting and praying for a miracle, a large corporation came in and bought that same piece of property. It was devastating to the church.

They had spent so much time praying and believing that this would be their new location. A year went by and they had no new direction − they didn't know what to do. Then, out of the blue, they received a call from a representative with the corporation that had bought the land they had so badly wanted. He told the pastor that they had decided not to build on the property and wanted to know if the church would still be interested in that land. The church bought the land they had originally felt God leading them to but at half the price they would have paid the year before – which was a savings of millions of dollars.

> *why don't amazing things like that ever happen to me? Where is our miracle?*

Sitting in the backseat of that jeep, listening to that story, I was thinking, "That's great. But God, why don't amazing things like that ever happen to me? Where is our miracle?" At that very moment the pastor telling the story turned around and pointed his finger at me and said, "And God is about to do the same kind of miracle for you and your congregation." His words shot through me like a lightning bolt. I physically felt something. It was like the "gift of faith" had been imparted to me. In a split second I knew, I just absolutely knew without any doubt, we were about to experience something amazing from God.

The day I arrived back home from Africa, I received a call from a realtor we had been working with. He said, "I couldn't wait for you to get back. I want to show you a piece of land." It was twelve acres right off the interstate in an area known as Renaissance Center.

It was on the market at a remarkable price of one million dollars. It was owned by the union and the only stipulation was to use union laborers in the construction. The name of this area, Renaissance, means revival or rebirth. What an incredible sign from God!

Our membership was overwhelmingly in favor of purchasing the property and within a short few months we entered a stewardship campaign. Everyone in the church was encouraged to make a financial sacrifice for the next three years. The congregation was small but highly energized and pledged one million dollars.

I knew absolutely nothing about construction, so I put together a building committee and started to look into architects and contractors. In my mind, I thought, "Let's build something!" I had no idea the level of due diligence that first had to be addressed.

Several months later we officially closed on the land and we were the new owners of the Renaissance property. We immediately put our current property up for sale, which was debt-free. We needed someone to purchase our building, which would be the down payment on our new facility.

We set up trips to Dallas and Houston to visit church facilities that were the same size as the facility we wanted to build. We gathered a tremendous amount of ideas and information after talking to pastors and staff members who had recently gone through building programs.

The first meeting we had with our architects was the dream stage of designing our new facility. It was an all-day meeting where our church staff gathered and we were told to dream of what the ultimate facility would look like if money wasn't a factor. I remember thinking the approach seemed crazy – I can dream a really big dream – but I also knew that we were working with a shoestring budget. The two didn't match up to me, and I wondered if we were wasting our time creating a fantasy instead of a reality.

Well, when we had finished that afternoon, we had scratched out a magnificent facility. What they designed was nine million dollars and that wasn't reasonable. We needed to grow in numbers and finances, but most of all we needed to sell our building. All we knew to do was to wait – wait for a miracle.

One year later we set up a tent on the Renaissance land and invited our church to come out for a prayer meeting – asking

God to help us financially and bless our endeavors. We desperately needed God's help. Because of the economy, the cost to build our new facility had now increased to ten million dollars.

Another year passed and we still had no prospective buyers for the building we were currently in. Building costs at that time were skyrocketing. Drywall and concrete prices had gone through the roof and were at an all-time high. We were absolutely frozen. This made no sense. Instead of God leading us forward, we were going backwards. Now, three years after purchasing the land, the plans the architects had originally designed had gone from nine million dollars to fifteen million.

This left us stunned. What made matters worse is that we hadn't had one offer on our building in three years. We met with the architects to start making cuts and somehow get this within a reasonable budget. Frustrations were mounting from every side as the economy worsened day after day. The union had sold us the property to generate union jobs. The architects were weary in all of our delays, redesigns, and continued cuts. In a very heated meeting with the architects, the union representatives, and our team, they demanded us to make a decision. They told us that our building was increasing in price by $100,000 a month. "Are you going to pull the trigger or not?" We were at a standstill. Our existing facility had to sell before we could do anything. It was a stalemate.

Five years had now passed. The architects went back one last time, cutting everywhere possible, until our dream facility was nothing more than an ugly square box. They eliminated the youth auditorium, downgraded all the interiors of the building and shrank the foyer to almost being nonexistent. Also, the parking lot had been downgraded from asphalt to gravel. The square footage was now not much more than our existing building.

This is where we were at after all these years. No one to buy our building and the facility we could afford was not worth building.

The amount of agony, stress, energy and money we all had put into this project was outrageous. It had consumed our building committee and me for years.

We called one last meeting with all parties involved. We told the union we could not afford to build on that property and we needed them to buy it back from us. That day we pulled the plug on a project we had worked on for six long years. That night, as I drove home, I felt nothing but despair. We had raised a million dollars and almost all of it had been spent trying to make this project work. My only thought was of all the people in our church who had sacrificed financially toward this endeavor. I knew people who put off buying a car to give to our building project. So many people had sacrificed deeply and now we had nothing to show for it. We had no property, no new facility, and the one million dollars we had raised was almost completely gone. I was so overwhelmed by the guilt of leading our people down a dead-end street. The pain and emotion was so intense that I had to pull my car off to the side of the road from crying so hard. I laid my head on the steering wheel, wept and asked myself, "How do you miss God this bad?! How do I ever explain a failure of this size?"

> *How do you miss God this bad?! How do I ever explain a failure of this size?*

The next morning I felt like I had a severe hangover. I've never experienced the real thing but I bet that's what it feels like. Driving to work that morning my face was puffy and my eyes were bloodshot. As I was driving I received a call from our realtor. When I saw that it was him, I hesitated to even answer the phone. I answered, and there was excitement in his voice, "Pastor, I want to show you a warehouse on the southeast side of town." My response was, "I'm not interested in a warehouse." He replied, "Oh, you're going to want to see this one!"

I reluctantly conceded to meet him, but I wasn't interested. I drove down Copper Avenue until it came to a dead end at this newly remodeled complex. I drove through a grand entrance with the words "Copper Pointe" overhead. As I drove toward the building it was stunningly beautiful. Millions of dollars had been spent remodeling the exterior of the facility, including a redesign of landscaping, decorative lighting and parking areas. The inside was just a huge hollow space. I was so intrigued by the possibilities but deep down I knew this was far beyond our means. As I walked through this huge empty space I noticed that the ceilings were fifteen feet high, but for some strange reason they had raised the roof in the center of the building to thirty feet. A few days later we took our original plans which the architects had drawn years before and laid them over the footprint of this new building – it fit like a glove. Right where the auditorium would be located is where the roof had been raised to the exact height of thirty feet that our original plans had specified, allowing for stadium seating.

When negotiations began, it was at the worst point of the economic crisis. All construction had come to a complete stop and loans were almost impossible to obtain. In our first conversation with the owners of this warehouse property, I told them their price was a million dollars too high and immediately they dropped the price by a million dollars. Our current property had been on the market for six years and I told him our dilemma. He said, "I will take it as a trade at your asking price and you can remain in it until you're ready to move in to this new facility." This was all moving so fast it made my head spin.

I explained to him that we would have to lead our congregation into a capital giving campaign to make this project work. Without hesitation he said, "To speed things along I will give the first gift of $250,000." And he did!

I Own A Very Expensive Suit

We had hired a building consultant from Atlanta, Georgia, and at this point he was working feverishly to secure a loan. This size of loan had been almost completely shut down across the country. Banks weren't lending. Our consultant had one lead on a bank that was considering our project. We had come so far and now everything was riding on the approval from this bank. Our consultant, being from Atlanta, was familiar with a far different culture than the culture we have in Albuquerque. Every time he came out he was all dressed up and we were always in jeans with untucked shirts. When he lined up our meeting with the loan committee from this bank, he told us that he wanted us to make sure we dressed in expensive suits. I told him I didn't think that was necessary, but he put his foot down and said we had one shot at this and that what he said goes. Well, that afternoon we were being fitted for suits. Expensive suits! And they looked incredible.

A few days later we drove up to the bank, which was in a small New Mexico town, in a black Yukon. We all stepped out of the vehicle looking like New York bankers – carrying stylish briefcases as we entered the bank. We walked through the lobby and everyone literally stopped what they were doing and stared as we walked by. We were ushered into the boardroom and waited to meet these powerful businessmen who were going to determine our future. After a moment the doors suddenly opened and two young guys walked in wearing jeans, t-shirts, and tennis shoes. I looked at our consultant and burst into laughter...and I couldn't stop. He was kicking me under the table, reminding me

ptytrript

that this was serious. But all I could think of was how silly we looked and how much money we had spent. A little later I slid a note to him that said, "Hey, while you're asking for loans, can you also request one to cover these suits?" He didn't think it was nearly as funny I did. I was just trying to lighten mood. In the end, maybe the suits really worked, because we got the loan that everyone said we would never get.

Standing In The Rain

What I realized after all these years was that God had put us in a holding pattern. God had made our progress on the Renaissance project absolutely impossible until the remodeling of Copper Pointe was completed, also giving time for us to grow and mature as a church. I know it's strange, but God seems to know more than we do.

> I know it's strange, but God seems to know more than we do.

Throughout all of the years of failures, ups and downs, victories, and disappointment, my biggest supporter and encourager was my dad. So many times, after coming out of meetings hearing more bad news and derailment, the first person I wanted to talk to was my dad. No matter how bad the news, he always had a calmness in his voice, and his unwavering assurance in God always brought me peace.

One of the monumental moments in my life was when I stood before the greatest people on the planet, and announced, "It's finalized! We own Copper Pointe and building starts immediately!" I couldn't wait to get home and call my dad to tell him the great news. "Dad, we did it! It really happened! After all these years!" And I couldn't wait to hear his response.

On that Sunday morning at the end of the service, I made the announcement. The excitement was so high that it felt like electricity in the air. As I left the stage, the church was erupting in applause. I stepped off the stage to the front row and I can remember how exhausted I was after completing five highly emotional services. As I reached my seat, I was met by some of my closest friends who quickly escorted me away, which was very unusual. They took me to the back parking lot where a car was waiting. Standing with them in the rain, I knew something was very wrong. That's when they informed me that my father had just died from a heart attack. In an instant, I had lost my best friend and my greatest encourager. All I could think was that I wouldn't be able to make that phone call that I so badly had wanted to make – that conversation would never take place. The best day and the worst day all collided in that one moment. The highest high and the lowest of lows created a mountain of emotion. The people standing around me were talking but I was unaware of what they were saying. I was a million miles away.

I remember looking up as the rain was falling and somehow it seemed to bring a peace to the moment. I also knew, as I stood there, that my dad was in the place he had talked so much about – he was in Heaven! A few minutes later, I was joined by my wife and three boys. As we stood together in that very solemn moment, no one knew what to say. And really, nothing needed to be said. The presence of the people you love the most is all you need. Kay had gone home during the last service and packed a suitcase for me. She knew I would want to be with my mom as soon as possible. One of our staff members wanted to drive me to my parents' home, which was several hours away. That was an act of kindness I will never forget. Kay and the boys stayed in Albuquerque to take care of all the details for us to be out of town and then joined me the next day.

It's moments like these that you really understand the enormous benefit of knowing Christ. We hear people talk about it all the time, but the peace we experience, even in the valley of death, is hard to explain. I'm just thankful that I know the Prince of Peace!

While waiting all of these years to build our new church, I continued to constantly dream. Every day I was dreaming and planning and envisioning what the new facility would look like. Every time I walked into a hotel lobby, restaurant or coffee shop I would measure their floor space and the size of every room. I analyzed why some places feel cold and uninviting while other places felt warm and comfortable – making you want to stay awhile. Each time I found an environment like that, I would pray, "Let our new church feel and look similar to this." When I walked into the lobby of a large movie theater in town, I would step it off, measuring the size of the room. I sat in that lobby many times praying, "God let us have a lobby like this when we build." That was the ultimate dream, while every architect and builder said it was impossible with our budget. My iPad was full of pictures, of modern building designs, decor and furnishings, that I had taken all over the country. I was making sure I was doing everything possible on my part, while waiting on God to do what we could not.

At the very time we were about start the interior design of our building a couple began attending our church who were some the greatest designers in the country. They were a gift from God. They donated hundreds of hours to bring the interior design to a level we could not have imagined. When we completed the plans and construction had begun, our atrium was three times larger than that of the movie theater in which I had sat dreaming so many times. There is now a sprawling atrium with a large coffee shop and fireplace, comfortable seating throughout, and a spiral staircase going up to the office complex with a landing overlooking the atrium.

The day they started framing the first walls I stood there almost in disbelief. It had been a grueling seven years fighting for the vision and now it was physically appearing.

Homeless Man Or Angel

So many miracles took place throughout the construction process but I want to share with you one of my favorites.

When we were coming to the end of the project we had a few large items go over budget and we needed to cut out a hundred thousand dollars. In a meeting to decide what to cut out of the building, there were two expensive items in the sound, lighting, and video budget that we decided we had to keep and couldn't live without. The rest of the cuts were being focused on the décor of atrium – the very thing I had worked on for years, creating the right atmosphere. They wanted to cut a portion of the coffee shop, take out the fireplace, and eliminate the spiral staircase and other decorative elements. I knew this was going to compromise the purpose of the atrium, the warm atmosphere, the "feel" and ambience of the building.

I drove back to our old building, where we were still having church, and was agitated as I walked in the front doors. A couple of staff members were standing there and I unloaded on them with all of my woes. I told them that I had to raise twenty thousand dollars within three days to keep the fireplace and a portion of the coffee shop that ties everything together. As I was telling that story, a man walked into the foyer. He was missing a leg and was poorly dressed. I just knew that he had come to ask for financial assistance (I know a homeless person when I see one). So I walked over and asked how I could help him. He said, "I've been attending here for the past few months and it's been a tremendous blessing to me. I just wanted to know if the church is in need of any money." I grinned and said, "As a matter of fact, today we are in great need." He replied, "Well then, I would like to write a check to the church." I thanked him for his kindness as he proceeded to write it out. In my mind I was thinking, "Maybe twenty dollars? No, at best it's fifty dollars." He ripped out the check, folded it and handed it to me. Then he turned and hobbled out the door. I didn't even bother to look at the check. I walked into the office and was talking to other staff members when I finally opened it up. I was speechless! It was written for the exact amount that I was just complaining about having to raise just a few minutes before. The check was for $20,000!

Nine months later our new building was completed in record time! Which was a good thing because the very next day was our grand opening. We had hundreds of volunteers franticly working all day trying to get everything cleaned and organized. Teams of people were there getting ready for the biggest day in the history of our church.

As I looked around and watched all of the people working, I noticed that the ones who had been working the longest and hardest were the remnant of people who had walked this entire journey with me. They had walked through the horrendous church split, the agonizing ministry elimination, and had sacrificed greatly during the two capital giving campaigns. They had stood with me through seven long years of talking about a new facility, being met by one disappointment after another. Standing there that day, I knew that these faithful, committed few were the real heroes. They were and are a rare breed, and I'm honored to have had the opportunity to stand with and labor beside them. I don't know what it is that makes some people so loyal and faithful, even through difficult times, but I'm thankful that our paths crossed, because it would have been impossible to accomplish the extraordinary without them.

After a long and exhausting day, and after everyone had gone home, I realized I was the last person in the building. As I approached the front doors I couldn't bring myself to leave. Finding myself lingering in the front entry I turned around and started walking. I walked through the foyer that flowed into the atrium and onto the auditorium. I strolled slowly, soaking in and enjoying the moment of absolute solitude, which is something I had not experienced in months. I will cherish that moment for the rest of my life. As I walked through the building I felt like God was walking right beside me. It was truly a sacred moment. I stood there shaking my head in disbelief and wondered to myself how I got here. Tears flowed down my face. The only words that would come out of my mouth were, "He is able to do far beyond all that we ask or think." This was a verse I had memorized as a young boy and quoted many times, but this was really the first time I quoted it with real understanding. I was standing in a new multi-million dollar building that was opening the next day.

That weekend we had over four thousand in attendance and several hundred gave their lives to Christ. The next weekend we baptized just over two hundred people. Those two weekends made me understand that dreams are not simply for those the world deems as exceptional but for *everyone* who has a dream.

Today, I enjoy looking into the past and remembering all the obstacles and difficult days because it always brings a smile to my face.

When all the teachers said I couldn't and church people said I wasn't talented enough, when angry people walked out the church doors never to return, and when I didn't believe I was good enough; when builders and architects said it was impossible and when the economy took a dive, when every realtor failed in their attempts and when bank loans were unattainable; when everybody believed I was just a foolish dreamer, out of touch with reality, that's when we were right where God wanted us to be – totally dependent on Him and perfectly positioned to see the greatest miracle of our lives.

The battle you're facing today is merely an attempt of the enemy to defeat you through his unrelenting taunts and intimidation. "The Lord says to you, do not be afraid nor dismayed…for the battle is not yours, the battle is the Lord's." Did you hear that? The battle is the Lord's! That simple truth is the difference between victory and defeat.

> *The odds may not be in your favor, but God is.*

The battle is not about you, it's all about your God – your God being big enough, strong enough, caring enough, and faithful enough to fulfill your dream and His promise. The odds may not be in your favor, but God is.

When our youngest son, Brandon, was seven years old, we enrolled him in swimming lessons. The first day, when all the kids got into the pool, they were hanging on to the ledge for dear life and were not sure if they were going to enjoy this experience. Their first instruction was to hold on to the ledge and dip underneath the water. This turned into mayhem. These seven-year-olds were spitting water, crying, wailing and begging to get out of the pool. It was absolutely chaotic. As I looked to the opposite end of this Olympic-sized pool I saw parents with infants getting into the water. I thought, "Surely they're not going to try to teach babies to swim. After all, it's an absolute disaster trying to teach seven-year-olds." I had to see this for myself. So I walked to the other end of the pool where these moms were in the water with babies, all under the age of six months.

As they held their babies out in front of them, the instructor told them to turn loose and let their babies sink underneath the water. Of course, these moms were very apprehensive and they were afraid to let go. It was stressing *me* out! I found myself wanting to yell, "Don't do it!" Eventually, one at a time they began to let go and their babies sank several feet beneath the surface of the water. Then, all of a sudden, they floated to the top and broke the surface like little corks. They took in a deep breath of air and flipped over on their backs, floating without any assistance. It was amazing! The instructor said, "I told you there was nothing to worry about. We were created to float."

> *I told you there was nothing to worry about. We were created to float.*

As I stood there those words rang in my ears, "We were created to float." What an incredible thought! We were designed by the creator not to sink, but to float to the top in every area of life. What's so exciting for all of us is that right now we are all writing the next chapter of our lives. What you are doing today will one day be *your* story to tell. When you mix your dreams with God's miraculous power, no doubt it will be a story people will talk about for years.

So go ahead. Do something risky. Take the plunge and enjoy rising to the top.

The End

CPSIA information can be obtained
at www.ICGtesting.com
Printed in the USA
FSOW01n1605050215
5061FS